Shells

and shell collecting

Shells
and shell collecting
S. Peter Dance

HAMLYN
London · New York · Sydney · Toronto

Published by The Hamlyn Publishing Group Limited
London . New York . Sydney . Toronto
Hamlyn House, Feltham, Middlesex, England
Copyright © The Hamlyn Publishing Group Limited 1972

ISBN 0 600 39259 7

Phototypeset by Photoprint Plates Limited, England
Printed in Western Germany
Mohndruck Reinhard Mohn OHG Gütersloh
Mohn Gordon Ltd, London

Contents

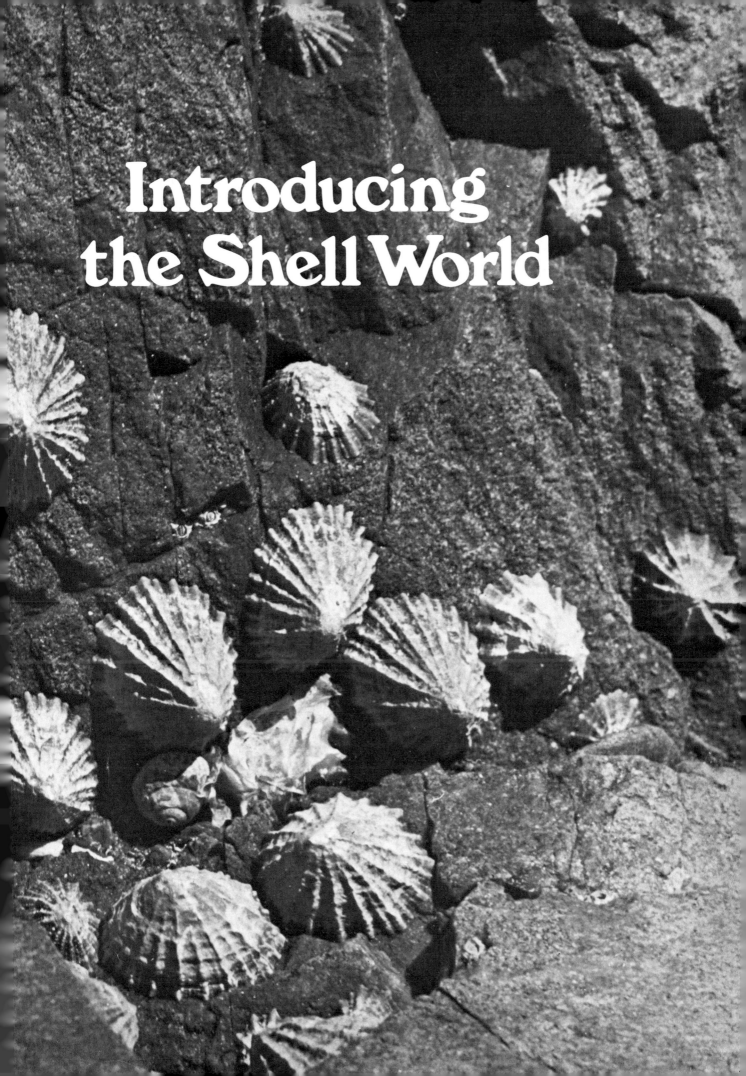

Introducing the Shell World

'Shells are at once the attraction of the untutored savage, the delight of the refined artist, the wonder of the philosophic zoologist, and the most valued treasures of the geologist'. So wrote a keen student of shells in the early years of Queen Victoria's reign, and his words are as true now as they were then. The popularity of shells is of ancient origin although different peoples have appreciated them in different ways. Obviously the 'untutored savage' is unlikely to find them satisfying in the same sense as the 'philosophic zoologist'. Nevertheless it can be shown that human beings widely separated from one another culturally and geographically often respond to shells in similar ways.

One shared response is the desire to collect them. Another is a tendency to eat some of the animals which live in them. Yet another is a compelling urge to arrange them, either in a decorative manner on the person, or in more or less orderly fashion in suitable receptacles. For one reason or another shells attract and please almost everyone, and at no time in the history of the world have they ever attracted and pleased more men and women than they do now. In this book we shall try to discover why it is that we are so captivated by the external skeletons of soft-bodied creatures low down the evolutionary scale.

Before we do so, however, it is essential to learn something about the creatures which make shells and live inside them. The term 'shellfish' is commonly used to denote a number of different kinds of sea creatures having hard, external skeletons. These include crabs, lobsters, shrimps and other animals totally unrelated to those in which we are exclusively interested. Our creature, which consists of a hard shell and a soft body, is known as a mollusc (meaning soft-bodied). With very few exceptions there are no hard parts of substantial size apart from the shell itself.

Molluscs, taken collectively, conform to no particular shape and they often adapt themselves to the nature of the habitat in which they live. It is their essential softness rather than their apparent hardness which has enabled them to adapt to so many different circumstances. They have survived because they are soft and plastic, not because they have evolved hard and unyielding shells. Molluscs are found almost everywhere: in the abyssal depths of the world's oceans, on the tops of mountains, among coral reefs, in stony deserts and leafy forests, in the mud of small ponds and huge lakes, and in the rushing waters of tiny streams and mighty rivers. They vary in dimensions from creatures the size of a pin's head to monsters of sixty feet or more in length. Some are fixed in one spot throughout life; others spend nearly all their

Acorn barnacles uncovered by the receding tide. These were once thought to be molluscs but are actually arthropods.

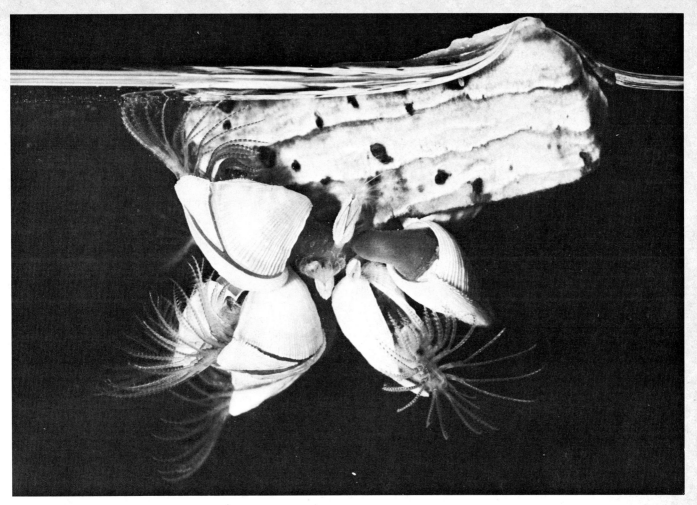

Goose-necked barnacles with their feathery tentacles extended

time darting about like underwater butterflies. Some eat very little; others never stop eating. Many are quite harmless, but there are numerous molluscs which are dangerous even to vertebrate animals. Some have elaborately sculptured and brightly coloured shells; others have no shells at all. With approximately 90,000 species, the group (or phylum) Mollusca is exceeded in numbers only by one other animal group, the phylum Arthropoda, which includes insects, spiders and crustaceans. In the entire animal kingdom there is no comparable collection of creatures so diverse in size, appearance and habits. Consequently, we ought to look for some characteristic features common to all molluscs by which they may be immediately recognized as such.

The most conspicuous and most characteristic feature, is not, as might be expected, the shell. The molluscan shell may be the hallmark of the Mollusca, and it is certainly the most distinctive, enduring and familiar part of those molluscs which have one, but many molluscs do not possess a shell. So we must still ask: what makes a mollusc a mollusc? This simple question is not easily answered. The most accurate, but least satisfactory, definition would be: a mollusc is a creature which cannot be allotted to any phylum other

than the Mollusca. This is not very helpful, even though there are several things common to many molluscs which are unknown or are barely perceptible in animals belonging to other phyla. The possession of a shell enclosing, or sometimes enclosed within, an animal usually points to that animal being a mollusc; but barnacles and lampshells (or brachiopods) are animals enclosed within shells too, and it is only when one looks at the non-shelly parts of these animals that their non-molluscan attributes are obvious.

A remarkable feature of molluscan development is the formation at an early stage of a particular larval form, known as a trochosphere, although this type of larva is common to animals of one or two other phyla as well. With the formation of the succeeding larval stage, the veliger or free-swimming stage, we have a developmental process peculiar to molluscs. But, since many molluscs do not pass through that stage there has to be something else which makes a mollusc indisputably a mollusc. The majority of them have a peculiar rasping organ called the radula. Unknown in other animals, the radula is so important a feature that it has been used to a great extent in the classification of molluscs. It will come as no surprise, however, to learn that many molluscs do not possess this uniquely molluscan organ.

It must be regretfully concluded that no single characteristic is shared by all molluscs: hence the

difficulty in finding a simple definition for them. In practice the biologist decides that a creature is a mollusc if it exhibits one or more of those features which are not exhibited by creatures of other phyla. If it has a veliger larval stage, or a radula, or both, it is a mollusc. If it exhibits features known to be associated with creatures possessing those salient ones, or others of comparable importance, it is still a mollusc. This is, of course, an over-simplification, but it does show that the definition of a mollusc is not easily given.

On the other hand, most people recognize a molluscan shell for what it is: a hard, brittle object which forms a protective covering for a soft-bodied animal. Whether it is in one piece or more, whether it is spirally coiled, cap-shaped, flattened, sculptured or smooth, colourful or colourless, they know that it is a shell. Instinctively they pick it up, handle it, and sometimes keep it. Some are so beguiled by it that they look for more, and when that happens they have introduced themselves to conchology, the study of molluscs and their shells.

Although it may be half hidden under a remarkable array of accessory processes the molluscan animal consists basically of a head, a foot, and a visceral mass. In the more advanced forms, such as most land, freshwater and marine snails, the head is well developed and bears tentacles, eyes and a mouth. To enable the animal to scrape away at food substances the mouth may be furnished with a jaw plate. Within the mouth the radula, consisting of few or many teeth, set in rows on a flexible ribbon of tough tissue, has a similar purpose but functions differently. Bivalves (molluscs with two-piece shells) lack heads and consequently are without jaw plates and radulae. The foot is that part of the animal which is used for locomotion. In gastropods (molluscs with one-piece shells) it forms a rounded or oval disc. In bivalves it is a triangular or hatchet-shaped lobe and is used mostly for burrowing into sand or mud. The visceral mass contains the reproductive, excretory, digestive and circulatory organs.

The heart has two chambers, and the kidneys are paired. There is usually a stomach, which is connected by a tube to the mouth at one end and to the excretory orifice at the other. Enveloping the animal is a sheet-like covering of very thin tissue called the mantle. This organ secretes the shell and, at the same time, the pigments with which it is coloured. Between the visceral mass and the mantle lies the mantle cavity, in which are situated the gills. Many non-marine snails do not have gills and in these the mantle cavity functions like a lung, allowing the snails to absorb air directly.

Top Radula, or tooth ribbon, of Steller's Chiton (**Amicula stelleri**) *much enlarged*

Left **Acanthocardia tuberculata**, *a large cockle, with its foot extruded*

Opposite Egg mass of Common European Whelk (**Buccinum undatum**)

Most of the gastropod snails which possess gills secrete a hard accessory disc called an operculum. This is situated on the upper side of the foot when the animal is extended and plugs up the aperture partially or completely when the animal withdraws into its shell. It is the characteristics of the shell itself which provide the principal subject matter of the following chapters.

Reproduction is accomplished in different ways by different molluscs. Self-fertilization is fairly common, and one or two instances of parthenogenesis (the production of offspring without fertilization) are known. Most marine snails and all chitons (molluscs with eight-piece shells) are bisexual. Most other snails are hermaphrodites (they are male and female at the same time). The Slipper Limpet (*Crepidula fornicata*) begins life as a male, passes through a hermaphrodite stage and finishes up as a female!

The sexuality of bivalves is still not fully understood, many of them appearing to change sex from male to female and to true hermaphrodites. Water temperature and food supply can determine the sex of certain oysters. Some bisexual molluscs develop shells which vary in size and shape according to sex. The shell of the female is sometimes much larger than that of the male. This is to accommodate the female's swollen gonads or developing embryos. A good example of this difference in size can be seen in shells of the Common Spider Conch (*Lambis lambis*), but it is evident even in shells of much smaller species, such as the European Winkle (*Littorina littorea*).

After the eggs have been deposited development is fairly rapid. In primitive gastropods, such as the limpets and top shells, the eggs develop quickly into freely swimming trochophore larvae. A few hours later they change into veliger larvae. Veligers of many gastropods have only a brief free-swimming period and so they are rarely found in large oceans and deep water. Since their wanderings are thus limited to fairly shallow water around coasts and along continental shelves, an Australian limpet, for example, will have difficulty in spreading outside Australian waters. Some of the more advanced gastropods, however, have a much longer free-swimming period in the veliger stage and may drift great distances before further development continues.

Cymatium parthenopeum and *Ranella olearium* are allied species which apparently originated in the Mediterranean region, but they have been

collected alive from many other parts of the world. They, and their close relatives, can survive a long free-swimming period and propagate themselves at the end of it. Some veligers are large and float easily for long distances. Cowries, which have such veligers, are very widely distributed over the warmer regions of the globe. This explains to a certain extent why some gastropods have a world-wide distribution and why others are limited to a small area.

The further development of a mollusc usually involves the growth of a shell. As the animal matures it adds new growth to its shell at the growing edge, and usually no more is added once maturity is reached. The shell of an immature mollusc often has an unfinished look about it. It is thin, its coloration is less brilliant (though occasionally the reverse is true), its outer lip is unthickened, and it lacks the spines or fingers which project from the edge of the aperture in some species.

Molluscs do not all feed in the same way. The more primitive gastropods have a many-toothed radula with which they scrape up algae or tiny particles of food mixed with less digestible material, such as sand grains. This type of feeding is found in abalones (Haliotidae) and top shells (Trochidae) among others. More advanced gastropods, such as whelks (Buccinidae), rock shells (Muricidae) and volutes (Volutidae), are carnivorous and prey on animals which are alive, moribund or decaying. Many are cannibalistic. Carnivorous molluscs have very few teeth in each row of the radula. A very specialized group of carnivorous gastropods, comprising the cones (Conidae) and turrids (Turridae), make use of a

Opposite Edge-on views of the Edible Mussel (**Mytilus edulis**) *showing the mantle edges and siphons*

Below Harpoon-like tooth of the Magus Cone (**Conus magus**) *seen under magnification*

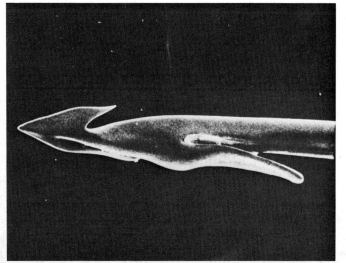

renewable, harpoon-like tooth to inject a narcotizing secretion into the bodies of their victims. In some cones the secretion is potent enough to be deadly to humans. There are numerous well-authenticated reports of human fatalities caused by cone 'stings'.

Since no bivalve has a radula or associated organs none of them is carnivorous. Most bivalves filter out the tiny particles of food suspended in the surrounding water and pass it, by way of the gills, to the stomach where it is sorted into digestible and indigestible pieces and processed accordingly. Among more specialized bivalve diets may be mentioned that of the shipworms (Teredinidae), which consists almost entirely of the wood through which they are constantly tunnelling. Squids feed on fish, crustaceans and occasionally each other. The octopus feeds mostly on crabs and other crustaceans. Giant squids, fearsome and insatiable carnivores, can tear a large animal to pieces in a few minutes.

Locomotion in molluscs is accomplished in several different ways. Most bivalves burrow but some excavate holes in rock or wood. Others flap their valves open and shut so that they flit about rapidly. Gastropods usually crawl or glide along on the broad foot, the constant discharge of a lubricating mucus making their passage easier. Some can swim by means of lateral flaps of mantle tissue. A few drift about aimlessly at the surface of the sea attached to rafts of their own eggs. Squids propel themselves by ejecting water from the mantle cavity through a muscular funnel. Many gastropods and bivalves are immobile throughout their adult lives. Some cement their shells to rocks and other hard surfaces. Some bore into rock and virtually entomb themselves. Others anchor themselves to things by means of a finely woven bunch of tenacious threads known collectively as a byssus.

It is not surprising that such diverse creatures, varying in size from the minute to the monstrous, living in almost every conceivable habitat, should have attracted universal attention for thousands of years. The focus of this attention has always been the shell itself rather than the animal which made it. This was natural, since the shell reflects many aspects of molluscan life and it frequently does so in the most exquisite fashion.

We shall be examining and comparing the shells of many different molluscs in a later chapter. Our examination will bring together shells of molluscs which have totally different modes of life. Shells of snails from the abyssal depths of the sea will be compared with those which live at the tops of trees. Shells of bivalves which cement themselves immovably to rocks will be placed side by side with those of bivalves which leap about with effortless ease. Abyssal or arboreal, anchored or free, they all leave behind their shells. We have abundant materials for our enquiry.

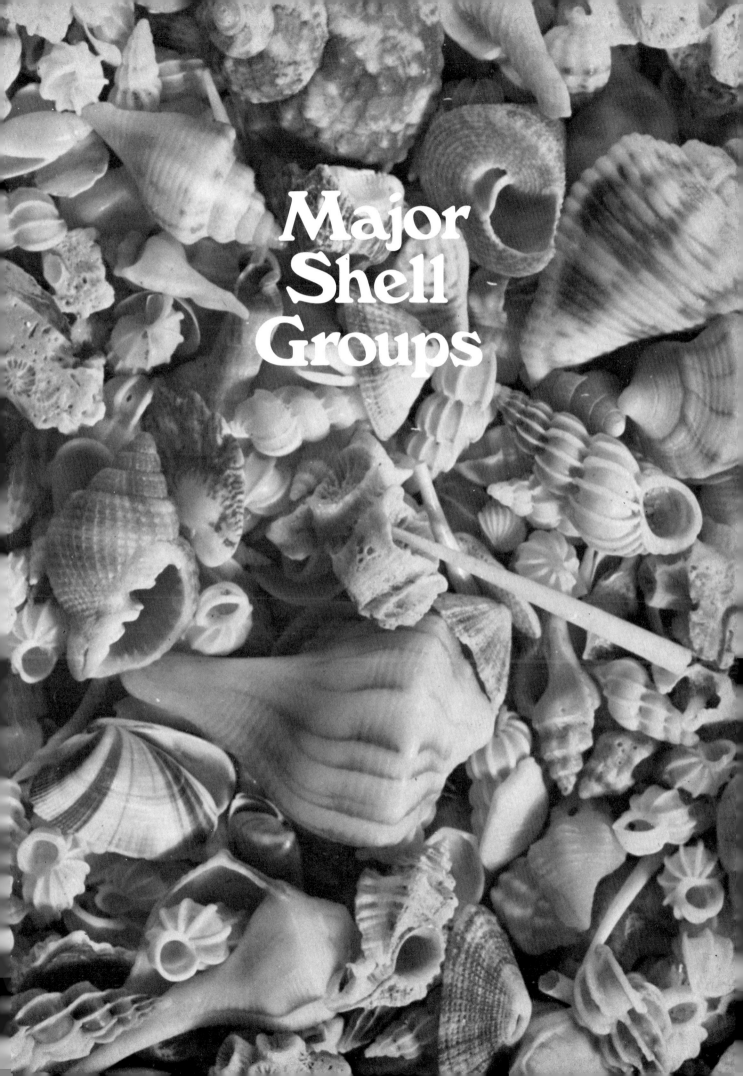

Major
Shell
Groups

The phylum Mollusca comprises six classes: Gastropoda, Bivalvia, Scaphopoda, Amphineura, Cephalopoda and Monoplacophora. Each class has representatives which are known only as fossils and each has members living today. With one or two exceptions, it is easy to decide to which class a mollusc belongs, even if it is a fossil. The Gastropoda is by far the most numerous in species, having more than the other five classes combined. Recent estimates of the total number of living species (including those yet to be found) vary from under 40,000 to more than 100,000, giving an average of 70,000. The Bivalvia, by a similar computation, number roughly 16,000 living species; the Amphineura 1,300; the Scaphopoda 1,100; the Cephalopoda 1,200; and the Monoplacophora 10. This gives a total of about 90,000 living species, or several thousands fewer than the number described by scientists during the past 200 years. Changing ideas on the nature of species have necessitated a revision of the estimated number from time to time.

The class Gastropoda (literally stomach-footed ones) comprises molluscs which secrete a one-piece shell and crawl on the disc-like foot. The shell may be coiled or uncoiled and may or may not cover the animal entirely when it is at rest. Some gastropod molluscs, such as the land and sea slugs, have no shell at all or, at most, a flattened calcareous plate which is situated inside the animal under the mantle skin. There are one or two species in which the shell is formed of two articulated pieces, as in the class Bivalvia.

Most gastropods have a radula, tentacles and eyes. The eyes may be situated at the base of the tentacles, at their tips, or somewhere in between. Some gastropods are blind. There is considerable variation in the radula from group to group.

There are three sub-classes of the Gastropoda: Prosobranchia, Opisthobranchia and Pulmonata. Though so different in form and habits they, or their ancestors, have all undergone a twisting of 180 degrees at a very early stage of development. This twisting action, known as torsion, is observable in the veliger larvae of prosobranchs. It must not be confused with the coiling of the shell, although the two activities may be closely associated. All gastropods, or their ancestors, have undergone torsion, but not all of them have coiled shells.

It is not fully understood why the gastropod animal goes through the process of torsion, and the subject cannot usefully be discussed here, but torsion has very important consequences for the mollusc. Basically, it alters the position of the visceral mass and some other organs in relation to

Below   The Spotted European Cowry **(Trivia monacha)** *is a gastropod. It is seen here under water crawling on its foot. The shell of this cowry is only about half an inch long.*

Above right   Living Ass's Ear from the south-west Pacific

Right   Top shell **(Zizyphinus zizyphinus)** *moving over compound sea squirts*

The Painted Top Shell is a gaily coloured species and has long tentacles

the head and foot. Organs that would otherwise be at the rear end come to adopt an anterior position close to those already in that position. It follows that the bulk of the animal is carried on its back, and a convenient way to support that bulk is to secrete a spiralling shell about it. Whether or not this is a satisfactory explanation of the coiled formation of gastropod shells, it is certain that coiling has been of great benefit to them. Moreover students and collectors generally agree that molluscs with coiled shells are much more attractive and interesting than those without them.

The sub-class Prosobranchia is the richest in species and individuals. The principal external feature by which its members are immediately recognized is the operculum. Though an accessory structure of relatively small size, it is sometimes elaborately sculptured and consequently of use in identification and classification. Internally most prosobranchs are characterized by the possession of gills. Included in this sub-class are both the largest and smallest snails in the world. Prosobranchs also account for nearly all of the most aesthetically pleasing shells and almost all of those which are considered commercially valuable as specimens.

The sub-class Opisthobranchia is noteworthy for having many species with much reduced shells or with no shells at all. When a shell is present it is often extremely thin and brittle; it is seldom thick. It may be attractive, sometimes extremely so, but more often than not it is exceeded in beauty by the animal, which frequently envelops it. No opisthobranchs and few other molluscs are more attractive than some of the sea slugs which, though they lack colourful shells, are often brilliantly coloured and exquisitely shaped. Unfortunately no sea slug retains its beauty after death; and, since it retains little else unless placed in a preservative, it is of no interest to the collector as a cabinet specimen.

The shells of certain opisthobranchs, however, are strikingly lovely objects, the colouring of some being scarcely equalled for brilliance and diversity of pattern by the shells of any other molluscan group. The opisthobranch shell is nearly always light and fragile because the possession of a thick and heavy shell would be a hindrance to a creature which swims or glides along as many of the opisthobranchs do. The closely coiled shells of prosobranchs are unlike those of most opisthobranchs, especially those of the bubble shells (*Bulla*), which seem to be made up almost entirely of one greatly inflated whorl (a whorl being one complete turn of the shell tube about a central axis).

The sub-class Pulmonata comprises those non-marine molluscs which do not have an operculum and do not have gills. The mantle cavity functions as an efficient lung enabling pulmonates to breathe air. The most familiar members of this sub-class are the snails and slugs of gardens, fields, forests, rivers, lakes and ponds, and they include some of the most highly evolved and successful molluscs in the world. Those snails and slugs which infest gardens and fields continue to multiply and spread in spite of man's constant war against them. In line with their success is their development of bodily structures which help them fill a large number of ecological niches: that is to say, they are able to colonize and thrive in situations which other animals would find uncongenial. These structures, in turn, are often reflected in their shells, which show almost as much diversity of form, sculpture and colour as those of the proso-branchs and opisthobranchs.

Nearly all of them crawl, or slide, on the broad, fleshy foot, a process made possible by a constant secretion of mucus which lubricates the foot. Some can fling themselves about with surprising agility and many can burrow. The slugs with shells (*Testacella*) habitually do so in their search for earthworms, but most other pulmonates burrow only to hibernate or to deposit eggs. The shells of the majority of pulmonates are thin and light, but some are so heavy that the animals have scarcely strength enough to move. The most successful land pulmonates are those which have been able to reduce their shells or do away with them altogether. Thus it is not surprising that slugs are so abundant, for without encumbering shells they can roam and ravage where their shell-carrying cousins cannot.

Ramshorn snail **(Planorbarius corneus)**, *a freshwater pulmonate*

The radula varies sufficiently from group to group for it to be an important element in classification, but it is basically similar in all. No pulmonate can show anything like the harpoon teeth of the cones, though some carnivorous species have long, sharp teeth enabling them to grasp and hold on to a wriggling prey.

The class Bivalvia, as the name suggests, comprises molluscs with shells composed of two pieces. Cockles, mussels and scallops are among the more familiar examples. All known species live in water or in close proximity to it. This implies a smaller number of existing species within the class than in the Gastropoda, simply because none has colonized the land. Even without this considera-

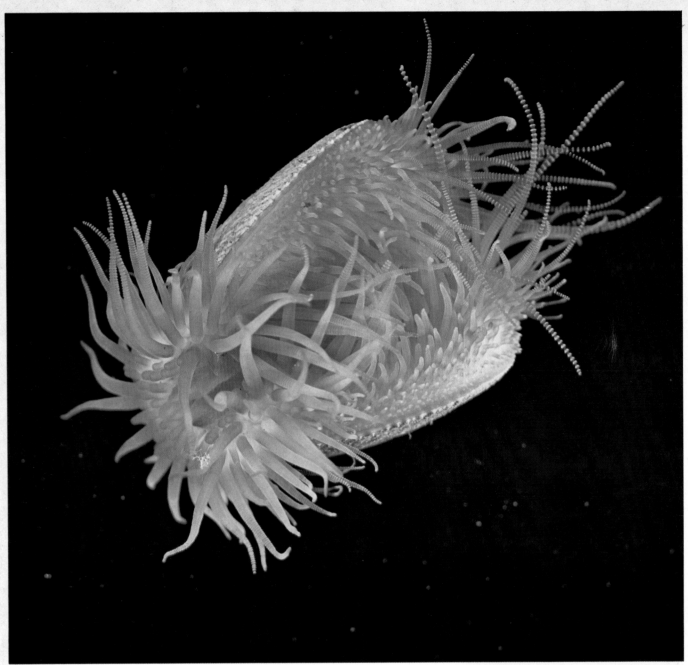

Above left   The colourful File Shell (**Limā hians**) *swimming underwater*

Left   Pheasant Shell (**Phasianella australis**)

Above   A strikingly patterned sea slug from an East African reef

tion, gastropods easily outnumber bivalves. If the most successful pulmonates are those which have dispensed with shells altogether, it follows that animals with two-piece shells are likely to be less successful (and consequently less numerous) than those with one-piece shells. In every way bivalves are simpler creatures than gastropods, though many find them equally fascinating as objects of study.

The possession of a shell consisting of two pieces is the principal feature of bivalves. Though this kind of shell does not help them to exploit the same wide range of environments as gastropods, bivalves are surprisingly versatile in their ways

and remarkably varied in their structure. Scallops dart about by rapidly opening and closing their valves. Awning clams (*Solemya*) swim by rapidly moving their foot like a piston-rod within the shell valves. A near relative of the sluggish oysters, the False Jingle Shell (*Aenigmonia aenigmatica*) can crawl on leaves out of water, rather like a gastropod; but the Giant Clam (*Tridacna gigas*) is so heavy that it is quite immobile.

Most bivalves have the two valves attached at one end or along one side by a strong ligament. Many have strengthened the attachment area by developing interlocking teeth along it. Prominent features seen on the inside of each valve are the

similar in shape, consisting of a tusk-like tube open at both ends: hence the popular name, tusk shells, by which they are generally known. The animal has no head, eyes or gills but it does possess a radula, and it usually has thread-like filaments with which to capture small organisms for food. All scaphopods live in the sea, sometimes at great depths, and nearly all of them bury themselves in mud with the narrow (posterior) end of the shell protruding up into the water. The shells of most species are very small and white, but a few are several inches long, and one or two are coloured.

Totally different in every way are the strange animals included in the class Amphineura. Known popularly as chitons, or coat-of-mail-shells, these primitive creatures have shells composed of eight pieces, are exclusively marine and spend almost all their time on or under rocks and stones. A radula is present, but the head lacks tentacles and eyes. Many species have light-sensitive organs in their shells. They are the only molluscs known to

Left   A Great Scallop **(Pecten maximus)** *with its valves gaping and the eyes round the mantle edge clearly visible*

Below   Living Pod Razors **(Ensis siliqua)** *showing protruding foot at right*

scars where the powerful adductor muscles are attached. These muscles close the valves, while the ligament provides the opening mechanism. Since the nature of its shell prevents the bivalve from coiling like a gastropod, it cannot assume such a variety of shapes, but it makes up for this by developing a wide range of variation in sculpture and colour. No gastropod shells can compare with those of the thorny oysters (*Spondylus*) for long and colourful spines, and no gastropod is more variable in colour and associated pattern than some of the scallops.

The class Scaphopoda (foot-diggers) is one of the smaller classes. The shell of each one is essentially

possess these. Binding the eight shell valves together is a tough, leathery girdle on which may be developed a variety of tiny spines or blunt knobs. In some the valves are much reduced in size and are quite inadequate to cover and protect the animal. Though few are brightly coloured many have striking colour patterns on their valves and girdles. The largest known chiton, *Amicula stelleri,* may reach twelve inches in length, but most species are much smaller.

The class Cephalopoda (head-footed ones) is also entirely marine and includes the octopus, squid and cuttlefish. The most active, powerful and intelligent of all invertebrates, the cephalopods

Above   A delicate bubble shell (**Hydatina**)

Above right   Mantle folds visible at the edge of a clam

Right   A sectional view of a Pearly Nautilus (**Nautilus pompilius**) *from the Pacific Ocean*

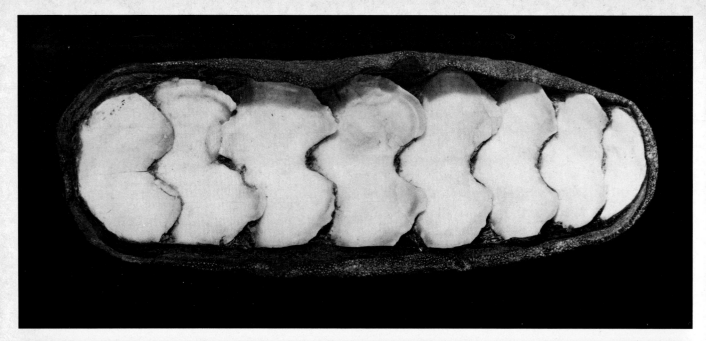

are far removed in both appearance and behaviour from all other molluscs. Most of the living species have a brain, a set of prehensile tentacles around the mouth with which to catch and hold the prey, a beak resembling a parrot's with which to tear the prey to pieces, large and well-developed eyes, and sometimes luminescent organs (for many species live in the regions of eternal night under the sea). The octopus has no shell, and the squid and the cuttlefish have only a rod-like or flattened bone-like structure inside. Only one group (*Nautilus*), still living in the Pacific, has an external protective shell. No cephalopod passes through a trochophore or veliger stage, but nearly all cephalopods develop a radula.

At the other end of the scale is the class Monoplacophora, until recently known only in the fossil state. About six living species are known, all of them so primitive in their structure that the coelacanth is modern by comparison. The shell of

Top The underside of Steller's Chiton **(Amicula stelleri)** *showing the eight overlapping shell valves*

Above The upperside of Steller's Chiton

Right Upper and lower sides of a cuttlebone

each living species is shaped like the bowl of a spoon and, without the animal in it, could be mistaken for a kind of limpet. But there the likeness ends, for the internal organs and gills are arranged serially and in pairs. This is an arrangement unknown in any other molluscs but is similar to that in many primitive animals of worm-like aspect. There are no eyes or tentacles, but there is a radula. Since the species live at great depths in the sea and only a handful of specimens has been collected, almost nothing is known of their life history.

Shell Shapes

That shells come in all shapes and sizes is obvious from the pictures in this book. To ask why they assume the shapes they do is rather like asking why eggs are egg-shaped: every three-dimensional object has to have a shape of some sort. It makes more sense if the question is re-phrased slightly— why do so many shells look similar?

A look at a typical, coiled gastropod shell shows that the aperture enlarges as the animal grows because the animal needs the extra room. The last complete turn (or whorl) is usually the largest because it has to house the greater part of the animal when it is stationary. If the shell has a very wide aperture it is probable that the occupant is too large to be accommodated comfortably in it. Similarly, the two valves of a typical bivalve shell are rounded in outline, more or less convex, and their edges are in contact all around when the animal withdraws into them. The two valves are seldom flat because the animal between them would be exposed permanently, and that is an unhappy situation for most bivalves. If the valves are very convex they are likely to house an animal which fills the space between them. Is it reasonable to assume, then, that molluscs with similar shells contain similar animals leading similar lives?

The shell of the abalone (*Haliotis*), which has a large body-whorl, contains an animal too large for it; but when it is on a smooth rock the animal can clamp its shell down and around it so that is is better protected. The beautiful shell of the Angel Wing (*Cyrtopleura costata*) is also not large enough to accommodate the animal which made it. As it lives most of its life buried in two or three feet of muddy sand it is seldom exposed to attack from large predators. It would usually be correct to assume that a mollusc with an abalone-like shell is going to resemble an abalone in many respects and may behave like one; a similar assumption regarding a shell like that of an Angel Wing would also be correct. Sometimes, however, such a supposition would be far from the truth. There are, for instance, many molluscs with limpet-like shells but they include unrelated species having totally different modes of life.

The variety of shell form in molluscs is apparently endless, but close examination shows that there are only a few basic forms. Three major groups may be distinguished easily: univalve (shell composed of one piece), bivalve (two pieces), and multivalve (more than two pieces). Indeed this was the basis of the classification of the Mollusca two centuries ago, but it has long been evident that this grouping is scientifically unsound. About

Upper and lower views of the Pana Shell (**Haliotis ivis**), *an abalone from New Zealand*

three quarters of molluscan species are univalved, but this group includes species belonging to four of the six classes comprising the phylum Mollusca: Monoplacophora, Scaphopoda, Gastropoda, Cephalopoda. The majority of the remainder are bivalved and belong to the class Bivalvia. (A few curious gastropods—*Tamanovalva* and *Berthelinia*—have two-piece shells, a peculiarity which has earned for them the name 'bivalved gastropods'.) The multivalved molluscs are all chitons belonging in the class Amphineura, although one or two kinds of strictly bivalved shells have accessory pieces of shell material which once justified their inclusion with the multivalves. The other animals which the earlier naturalists grouped with the multivalves are not molluscs at all. As this is not a treatise on systematic conchology we can take univalves, bivalves and multivalves in turn and compare the shells comprising each group regardless of their true evolutionary relationships.

The univalved group is easily the most numerous in species, displays by far the most variations of shell shape, and has representatives living in the sea, in inland waters, and on land. Bivalves do not live on land and all multivalves are marine. A striking feature of most univalves is their obvious asymmetry (which means that very few can be cut to produce two halves which are identical mirror-images of each other). Even those which look symmetrical are usually found to be otherwise when examined closely. Most limpets (*Patella*) and many other limpet-like shells are nearly symmetrical. In young limpets, however, the apex retains a coiled, larval shell which drops off before maturity. A perfectly symmetrical limpet is seldom found anyway because it must accommodate itself to the surface of the rock on which it lives and few rocks are flat and smooth. Other symmetrical univalves are the tusk shells (*Dentalium*) and the shells of *Carinaria*. The most exquisite and most familiar example of apparent symmetry is seen in the sectioned Pearly Nautilus (*Nautilus pompilius*). The only way symmetrical univalves can vary their appearance is by the development of different sculptural processes and by varying their colours and colour patterns. Fortunately the great majority of univalves tend to coil, and it is this tendency which has enabled them to develop such a wonderful diversity of shapes.

The simple cone is the fundamental shape of the univalve shell. Let us assume that we have a cone made of some plastic material which will adopt any shape we want. Extend the cone and perforate the tip, and it becomes like a tusk shell. Squash the

The Slipper Limpet (**Crepidula fornicata**) *which smothers and kills oysters*

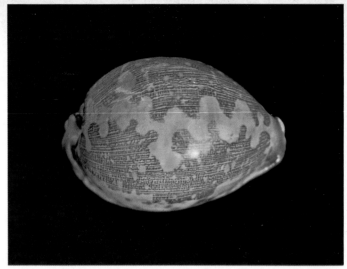

Right *The Map Cowry* **(Cypraea mappa)** *of the Indo-Pacific*

Below **Telescopium telescopium**, *a common inhabitant of swampy areas, has a strong central pillar or columella.*

cone flat and the resultant disc has some resemblance to the shell of *Umbrella,* which, in life, sits on the top of an animal and gives it almost no protection at all. Compress the cone laterally and it becomes a shell like the South African limpet *Cymbula compressa.* Pull out one side of the cone and it resembles the shield shells (*Scutus*) of the Pacific Ocean. Punch a hole in the top and a keyhole limpet (*Fissurella*) is the result; enlarge the hole and it becomes the Great Keyhole Limpet (*Megathura crenulata*). Cut a notch in the side and you have a slit limpet (*Emarginula*). Many freshwater and marine molluscs have shells which have adopted one or other of these shapes although no terrestrial mollusc seems to have produced a basically limpet-shaped shell.

Once a cone has been lengthened, raised, flattened, or laterally compressed, there is little else that can be done to alter its basic shape unless it is also twisted. Twist a cone so that it tends to form a descending spiral and immediately a host of new possibilities present themselves. A slight twist in a clockwise direction produces something like a cap shell (*Capulus*), and certain freshwater limpets (*Ferrissia*) have shells which are approximately this shape too. A beautiful example of a simple cone twisted still further without the consequent raising of a prominent spire is seen in some New Zealand molluscs (*Sigapatella*). These cling to rocks in the manner of limpets (to which they are not even remotely allied). At this point we have come to the end of the simple-cone series in which the base is quite open: from now on the shell is a spirally wound tube.

The tubular characteristic is not very obvious in many species. One would scarcely consider the shell of an abalone, with its disproportionately large aperture, to exhibit it; but it is undoubtedly spiral in its formation and coils upon itself about an imaginary axis. The conchologist says that such a shell 'expands rapidly'. Smaller versions of the 'haliotis shape' are seen in the shells of *Stomatia* and a few other marine shells. A tiny mollusc living just above high-tide mark on British and French coasts (*Otina ovata*) has just such a shell and this sits on top of the animal more like an odd hat than a protective shell. On land too there are molluscs which have a shell of similar shape. These are carnivorous slugs—they eat earthworms—and their shells are placed at the tail end. Since these slugs chase worms through their burrows their shells would be a hindrance if placed anywhere else. One of these slugs is named *Testacella haliotidea* in allusion to the haliotis-shape of the shell.

Here we have some good instances of how unrelated species living under very different conditions have evolved shells which have a strong superficial resemblance to one another. *Haliotis* is a fairly primitive marine mollusc which fastens itself to rocks and whose shell covers it

Capulus ungaricus (left) is a slightly twisted cone with a prominently raised spire while **Sigapatella novaezelandiae** *(right) has only a slight spire.*

when at rest. *Otina* is a tiny creature living in rock crevices or in old barnacle shells above high-tide mark, whose shell offers the occupant scarcely any protection. *Testacella* is a highly-evolved, slug-like creature whose shell is a mere appendage at its tail end.

When the aperture is not so open the shell is termed 'turbinate' (wound spirally about an imaginary axis in much the same way as a turban is wound about the human head). The majority of shells—marine, freshwater and terrestrial—are more or less turbinate in shape. The well-rounded, mostly smooth turban shells are typified by the Turk's Cap (*Turbo sarmaticus*). Essentially similar, however, are the shells of some freshwater molluscs such as the apple snails (*Pila*). If the base of a turbinate shell is flattened, as though by pressure from above, the resulting form is rather like a child's spinning top and again there are very many shells which conform to this shape. The marine top shells (Trochidae) vary considerably amongst themselves but they are always unmistakably trochoidal. If a shell resembles a top there is a very good chance that it will be a true top shell, particularly if it comes from the sea. On the other hand there are many non-marine shells which are trochoidal in shape, nearly all of them being terrestrial snails. Most of these live in tropical rain forests and are usually colourful. *Papuina hedleyi* is a striking example. Among freshwater shells, where the trochoidal shape is not common, good examples are found among the remarkable marine-like shells which live in Lake Tanganyika. *Chytra kirki* and *Limnotrochus thomsoni* are, as far as their shells are concerned, perfect analogues of the exclusively marine top shells. The presence of such shells in this lake (there are many others there which resemble marine shells) was for long a sufficient reason for scientists to believe that Lake

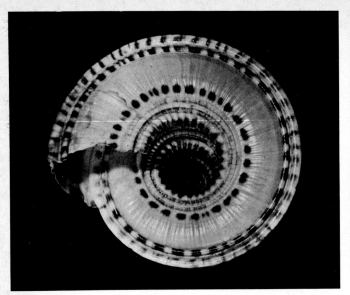

Upper and lower views of **Architectonica perspectiva**

Tanganyika was an inland sea which had been cut off from the Indian Ocean millions of years ago but which had retained an essentially marine fauna. Probably no one holds that belief now, or at least no one believes that the shells in it are the immediate descendants of true sea creatures. Flattening the trochoidal shell produces a series of shapes which can be matched, at one end of the scale in the beautiful stair-case shells (*Architectonica*), and at the other end in the freshwater ram's horn snails (*Planorbis*) and the very similar but unrelated *Marisa cornuarietis*. Some shells coiled on the flat, like *Planorbis,* have the whorls slightly unwound so that they resemble uncoiled watch springs.

Many univalve shells do not resemble any of the shapes described so far. Another series can be constructed consisting of species which are elongate rather than top-shaped. Many land shells native to South America and Africa resemble each other in their 'bulimoid' shape (so called from the scientific name *Bulimus* which used to be applied to most of them). The Pheasant Shell (*Phasianella australis*) and a West African volute (*Ampulla priamus*) show that this shape may be found among sea shells too. For a long time *Ampulla priamus* was believed to be a land shell because of its resemblance to one. Considerable enlargement of the body whorl results in a shape similar to that of the baler shells (*Melo*) which include some of the most voluminous shells in the world.

Thousands of different univalves are narrowly pointed and vary in size from objects barely visible to the naked eye to relative giants of six inches or more. The Marlinspike (*Terebra maculata*) and its relatives are large examples of this form, and the screw shells (*Turritella*) provide a similar series. Many land shells are very thin and elongate. *Rhodea, Columna, Obeliscus* and *Brachypodella*— all of them natives of South America—are good examples of extremely attenuated land snails which retain their spires throughout life. Some land snails of this shape lose some of their early

whorls because they are fragile and easily broken off. In freshwater there is an extensive family of snails living in tropical regions which includes very many species having narrowly pointed shells: these are well exemplified by the Black Melania (*Faunus ater*). Perhaps the most striking instance of resemblance between the shells of marine and non-marine molluscs is provided by one of these snails, the Variable Melania (*Melanoides variabilis*), which lives in rivers in India, and *Abyssochrysos melanioides,* which is found at a depth of a thousand fathoms in the Indian Ocean off the coast of South Africa. Even their opercula are similar. Experts have yet to discover any sound reason why these two molluscs should not be considered relatives of each other, although a close relationship seems unthinkable in view of their dissimilar homes and habits.

It would be difficult and perhaps monotonous to discuss the many other forms assumed by univalve shells but it is worth saying something about a feature of their growth which is common to most of them. Many organic structures exhibit spiral conformations: horns of certain mammals, molluscan shells, the chameleon's tail, the tongues of many insects, even locks of human hair. These curves are all examples of the 'logarithmic spiral' (also known as the 'equiangular spiral'). The most perfect examples of the logarithmic spiral in nature are formed of material which is inanimate and rigid (the chameleon's tail and insects' tongues are really nothing more than temporary attitudes of mobile material). Structures which display this kind of curve do not grow in the way that apples or human beings grow; they increase by adding new material to old, the latter remaining unchanged. Cats' claws and elephants' tusks are eloquent and familiar examples. The singular property shared by all such structures is their ability to change their size without changing their

Turritella terebra *is one of the longest of the tropical screw shells.*

shape. This is the essence of the logarithmic spiral. It is seen in a shell which widens and lengthens in the same unvarying proportions. The shell, like the contained animal, grows larger but its shape does not alter. What we have here is something which, no matter how much it grows, is always similar in shape to itself as it was at a preceding stage of growth, and as it will be at any time in its future. This can be seen very well by taking an abalone (*Haliotis*) and noting the successive growth stages. We see that all the stages are precisely similar in shape; only the overall size has changed.

A shell is nearly always illustrated in books with its aperture towards the observer or facing away from him, and this is usually how one inspects the shell itself. It is only when it is looked down upon from above its apex that its spirality is well seen. What all this means for the animal inside the shell is not obvious, but there is no doubt that the logarithmic spiral is a most economical growth curve which allows the animal to expand and grow with a minimum of effort and trouble. It also helps it to build a strongly constructed shell. Strangely enough it seems as though the shell curls the animal and not the animal the shell. This is clear from an examination of all of those molluscs which do not have a shell: not one shell-less mollusc is spirally coiled.

The logarithmic spiral is a prominent feature not only of the shell but also, sometimes, of the operculum which seals off the shell's aperture. Inscribed on the surface of many opercula are growth spirals which, in some instances, show a curved line of growth from the centre to the edge. In the thick and heavy operculum of the Green Snail (*Turbo marmoratus*) the successive increments of growth are built up along a beautifully curved line. How the animal overcomes the problem of ensuring that the operculum always fits snugly into the aperture of its own shell— which itself is constantly enlarging—is one of nature's miracles. If a shell is compared with its own operculum another interesting feature emerges. If the shell has a right-handed spiral that of the operculum is left-handed, and vice versa. This arrangement does not always hold good: some shells which are normally left-handed have opercula with left-handed growth spirals.

In the shell of the Pearly Nautilus (*Nautilus pompilius*) the logarithmic spiral finds its loveliest expression (although this can only be fully appreciated after sectioning it). It can also be found in some bivalves. The two valves of bivalves are usually joined together by a ligament and so it is not possible for them to exploit such a range of shapes as the univalves. But the logarithmic spiral is often represented in both valves of a bivalve at the umbonal end (the part from which all growth proceeds). Excellent examples are provided by the robust shell of the Heart Cockle

(*Glossus humanus*), which is unrelated to the true cockles, and the more delicate shell of *Corculum cardissa*.

There is less variety of basic form among bivalves than among univalves. Nevertheless bivalves have assumed many interesting shapes, from triangular and flattened to round and globular, long and narrow to short and bulbous. Perhaps a majority of bivalves have shells which are basically triangular in outline though none is exactly triangular. Wedge shells (*Donax*) are good examples of triangular-shaped shells. If a hypothetical triangular shell is pulled anteriorly and posteriorly at the same time we arrive at something like a razor shell (*Ensis*), so well adapted to burrowing rapidly in sand. If the triangle is rounded out to give us a fan shape we have a member of the scallop group (Pectinidae) which, by rapidly flapping the two valves open and shut, can propel itself through the water. Most of the known bivalve shapes are similar to or derived from one of these. Some have taken an independent line, however, and have ended up looking more like univalves. The watering-pot shells (*Brechites*) begin life conventionally with tiny two-piece shells, but later in their life history they develop a long tube open at one end and formed at the other into a structure resembling the 'rose' of a watering can. Only a tiny pair of valves cemented into the side of the tube is there to remind us that this is really a bivalve (although a brief examination of the living animal would leave no room for doubt). The destructive Ship Worm (*Teredo navalis*)—which is not a worm but a bivalve mollusc—has a strange relative, *Kuphus polythalamia,* living in mangrove areas of the Indo-Pacific. Its true shell is tiny in relation to the size of the animal, which can be over a foot long, but the animal also secretes a thick shelly tube in which it lives. The tube—all that is usually found of this mollusc—

may be two or three feet long, and it was many years before it was learnt that a bivalve mollusc forms it.

To appreciate the way in which most shells are constructed it is necessary to see inside them, and this can be done by examining them in cross section. The Pearly Nautilus is seen to be exquisitely chambered, and fresh shells have a hollow cord (the siphuncle) linking the walls of each chamber. In life the chambers would be filled with either a gas or a watery fluid, and by regulating the amounts of gas and fluid the creature can ascend or descend in the water at will. Only in cross section can you fully appreciate the perfection of its spiral formation. A longitudinal section through an auger shell (*Terebra*), however, shows a series of interconnected chambers wound about a central axis (the columella). A sectioned volute is remarkable for the plaits or columellar folds on the columella, while a sectioned cowry is seen to contain an earlier growth stage which is unlike the mature shell. A section through a cone or an olive shows that the earlier stages have been largely absorbed by the animal so that the innermost ones are paper-thin. In some gastropod shells (e.g. *Olivella* and *Nerita*) absorption of the inner shelly material proceeds so far that the shell is almost hollow inside. Molluscs belonging to a single generic group may include species which absorb more of their internal structure than others belonging to that group. The large Bubble Margin Shell (*Prunum bullatum*), for instance, does not absorb any of its internal structure, but the Spotted Margin Shell (*Persicula persicula*) does so to about the same extent that olives do. Bivalves have little of interest to show when sectioned because, in a way, they are sectioned already into two halves. A large species allied to the thorny oysters has valves which are formed in layers with wide spaces between them.

Opposite   Two unrelated bivalves, both commonly known as the Heart Cockle, have similarly formed shells. **Glossus humanus** *(left) is from European waters and* **Corculum cardissa** *(right) inhabits the Indo-Pacific region.*

Top   Variety of shape in bivalves is exemplified by the Great

Scallop, **Pecten maximus**, *(bottom right) the Abrupt Wedge Shell,* **Donax trunculus**, *(bottom left) and the Pod Razor,* **Ensis silqua** *(top).*

Above   Pennant's Top Shells **(Gibbula pennanti)** *showing opercula*

Shell
Sculpture

Most molluscan shells are ornamented, to a greater or lesser degree, with sculptural processes. Those from the depths of the world's oceans are less likely to be elaborately sculptured, perpetual darkness and scarcity of food (and consequently of shell-building material) contributing to the production of fragile, thin shells. Conversely, shells become more elaborately sculptured as the living conditions become more agreeable. It follows that those with elaborate processes (or high gloss) and rich colouring are the ones which live in shallow water in tropical regions.

The basic requirements for the production of a strong, colourful shell are sunlight, warmth and an abundant food supply. Thus, a shell's appearance gives a good clue to the nature of its habitat. Non-marine shells are also generally more attractive and more strongly built in warm, sunny environments than they are where conditions are less congenial, but it is not necessarily true, for instance, that freshwater molluscs produce more attractive shells in tropical places. Shells of freshwater molluscs are not very attractive—to human beings—under any conditions.

Before studying the different kinds of sculpture it is essential to say something about the composition of shells. The basic constituent of a shell is calcium carbonate which, in one form or another, comprises up to 98 per cent of the total inorganic matter. The skeletal structures of most animals, including our own bones, are also largely made from calcium carbonate. Covering the outside of most shells is a thin layer (the periostracum or epidermis), which is made of a horny material known as conchiolin, and this protects the shell against the action of corrosive chemicals present in the mollusc's environment. Conchiolin is also the main ingredient of many opercula and a small amount is present in the shell layers.

These substances are incorporated into a fluid secreted by the mantle, the thin, fleshy envelope which covers most of the mollusc's body. New shell growth is deposited along the mantle's free edge. In the course of its life a mollusc will sometimes deposit additional shelly matter onto the inner lining of a shell, and some species deposit thick additional layers at certain places on the outside. The solid shell is composed of thin layers of calcium carbonate, in the form of aragonite or calcite, welded together by small amounts of conchiolin. These layers vary in their crystalline structure. A nacreous inner layer forms the familiar mother-of-pearl lining, an outer prismatic layer lies under the periostracum, and a crossed-lamellar layer is sandwiched in between the two, giving strength to what would otherwise be a fragile shell. Each layer is deposited at the same time along the mantle's edge, but at different points on it.

Even an apparently smooth shell possesses a certain amount of sculptural detail. Minute pits or raised dots, incised striations or raised ridges, or combinations of these and other sculptural forms occur on many glossy shells. Some familiar shells, however, are smooth all over. Most cowries, olives and margin shells have smooth, highly polished surfaces without any sculpturing on them. Such shells acquire their shiny exteriors through being constantly enveloped in and lubricated by the folds of the mantle. These folds slide up and over the sides of the shell and meet along the back (or dorsum). Where they meet there is often a tell-tale marking on the shell and such markings are conspicuous features of many cowries. The Map Cowry (*Cypraea mappa*) is most strikingly marked where its mantle folds meet. Obviously spines, knobs or other shelly protuberances would be a hindrance to this kind of mollusc. At the opposite end of the scale are rock shells (Muricidae) and rock oysters (*Spondylus*), which are embellished with long spines. Between these extremes there is every conceivable sculptural variation.

The successive stages of growth of a molluscan shell are sometimes barely perceptible, but sometimes well marked. When growth is arrested for a relatively long time the shell may develop a prominent rib (or varix) which is virtually the edge of a fully formed aperture. Among the most beautiful of all gastropod shells is the Precious Wentletrap (*Epitonium scalare*), which has flange-like varices placed with great regularity all around the whorls.

It is instructive and fascinating to study the arrangement of varices on various kinds of gastropod shells. Apart from the Precious Wentletrap, there are many species with shells having prominent varices arranged in a regular way around the whorls. This indicates that they produce a varix at roughly equal intervals of time. The mollusc actually spends most of its growing time either dormant or building a varix. Relatively little time is spent constructing the material between the varices, which explains why such shells are seldom found without a fully formed apertural lip.

In some rock shells there are three varices to each whorl, which are in exact alignment across the whorls, as in the beautiful *Pterynotus alatus*. Viewed from above the apex, the varices tend to curve around in a clockwise direction. In the frog shells (Bursidae) and hairy tritons (Cymatiidae) the varices are also aligned across the whorls, but they are found only on alternate whorls. Some helmet shells (Cassididae) show various arrangements of varices according to the species. In one

Previous pages   Enlarged surface detail of Rumpf's Slit Shell

Above   Magnified view of the fine sculpture on a fossil shell

*Right   **Spondylus regius**, a colourful thorny oyster*

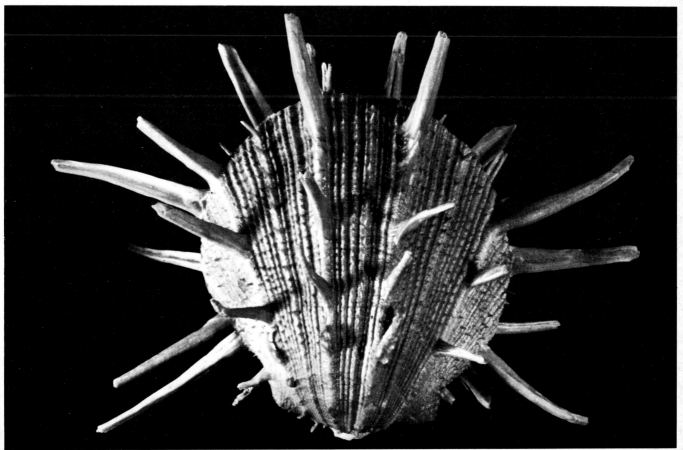

Above   The beautiful sculpture of **Latiaxis Kinoshitai** *from Japan is reminiscent of some Japanese architectural forms and could have inspired them.*

Right   The gaping valves of one of the world's most exquisite bivalves, the Angel's Wing **(Cyrtopleura costata)**. *It is difficult to collect since it lives an arm's length down in sandy and muddy substrates.*

Opposite   The Giant Frog Shell **(Bursa bubo)**, *a fairly common shell from coral reefs in the Indo-Pacific region*

the varices (viewed from above) are all parallel, in another they are at right angles to each other and in yet another they are aligned across alternate whorls.

When a shell has many well-marked growth stages these are described as ribs, although they may be formed in the same way as varices. Ribs are found on the shells of gastropods and bivalves and are usually parallel to the line of growth or at right angles to it. The Many-ribbed Harp (*Harpa costata*) is probably the most admired of all conspicuously ribbed shells, and the harp shells generally are noteworthy for the beautifully regular arrangement of their ribs. Among bivalves the Frilled Venus (*Bassina disjecta*) is of comparable beauty, its ribs following the line of growth and being drawn out to form thin frills.

A gastropod shell with prominent ribs at right angles to the line of growth is the New England Neptune (*Neptunea decemcostata*), and among bivalves the Ribbed Cockle (*Cardium costatum*)

shows this type of ribbing particularly well. Occasionally a shell has both types of ribbing. When they are of equal prominence they produce a lattice effect, as in the Magnificent Wentletrap (*Epitonium magnificum*) and the Basket Lucina (*Fimbria fimbriata*). Such shells are said to have a decussate (or cancellate) sculpture.

The most conspicuous manifestation of sculpture is seen on rock shells, rock oysters and a few other groups of spiny marine shells. Like other forms of sculpture, spines are secreted at certain points along the mantle's edge. In a spiny bivalve, such as the Royal Comb Venus (*Hysteroconcha dione*), the spines are secreted in pairs and the last to be added are the longest. In the Atlantic Thorny Oyster (*Spondylus americanus*) the spines on the upper valve are longer and more perfectly formed than those on the lower, cemented valve. There is only one freshwater bivalve which can be regarded as spiny—the now rare *Canthyria spinosa* of North America. This species has spines which stick out

Above **Cardium costatum** *exhibits strong ribbing.*

Below *The Royal Comb Venus* **(Hysteroconcha dione)**

Opposite *A spiny nerite,* **Clithon brevispina,** *from New Guinea*

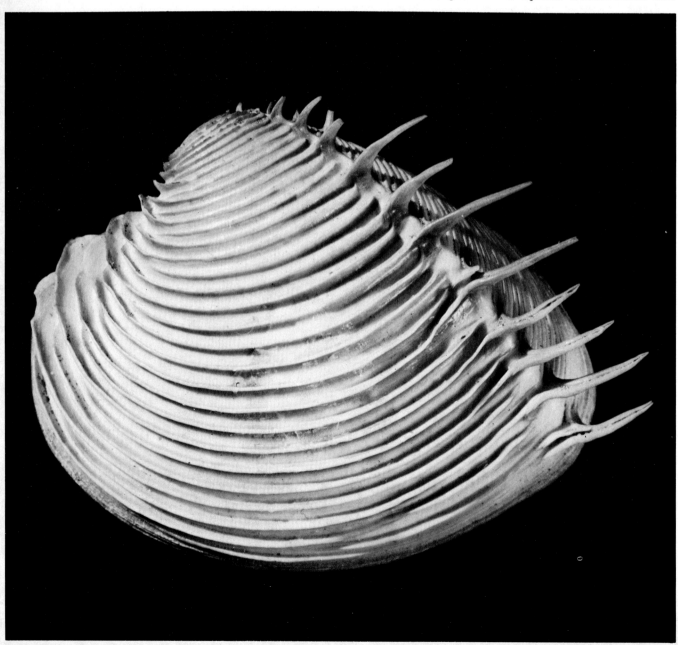

almost at right angles from the shell valves.

The most exquisite examples of spiny sculpture among gastropods are found on the rock shells. For centuries the Venus Comb Murex (*Murex pecten*) has been coveted by collectors, the many long, curved spines with which it is ornamented being unmatched for beauty in the molluscan world. Spiny whelks (*Tudicula*) resemble short-spined rock shells, and spines of comparable delicacy are found in a tropical marine nerite (*Clithon corona*). Long, stout spines are a distinctive feature of the genus *Guildfordia,* and in *Stellaria solaris* they radiate out in a manner reminiscent of the sun's rays. Some kinds of limpets, especially those from South African coasts, have shells whose edges extend into sharp points, but these scarcely deserve to be called spines. Scorpion shells are in no sense spiny when immature, but when fully grown they develop long and robust projections, or digitations, along the edge of the outer lip. These projections are so strong and thick that they seem scarcely comparable with the thin, easily fractured spines of rock shells, but they are formed in essentially the same way. Rock shells appear to be very different because they produce several sets of spines, whereas scorpion shells produce only one set.

Many land-snails develop spines on their shells, but nearly all the species are very small. Among the most remarkable and beautiful of all land snails are the species of *Opisthostoma* from Borneo and elsewhere in South-east Asia. Only two or three millimetres long, their shells are sometimes ornamented with long, curved spines. A few freshwater snails have spiny shells, the most noteworthy of these being *Tiphobia horei,* one of the many extraordinary species from Lake Tanganyika.

It is not clear whether the spines of a mollusc serve any useful purpose. Certainly, the spines of the Royal Comb Venus or the Venus Comb Murex would be a deterrent to certain predators, such as

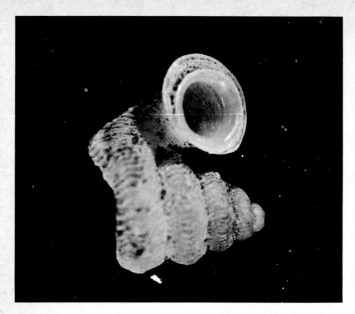

Opisthostoma pulchellum, *a curiously distorted shell from the interior of Borneo, is only some three millimetres long.*

fish and the larger molluscs. On the other hand, almost nothing will prevent starfish from making a meal off a tasty mollusc, no matter how well it is armed with spines. If, as seems probable, the most impregnable mollusc is one which has the longest, strongest and most numerous spines, it might have been expected that spiny shells would be more abundant than they are. It is just as likely, however, that the simple act of burial under sand and mud gives a mollusc at least as much protection as would a battery of spines.

It is not possible, in the space available, to discuss the many other kinds of sculpture to be found on the outside of shells. On the other hand, it is worth paying some attention to the sculptural characteristics on the inside surfaces of many gastropod shells. Usually these take the form of small rounded processes called denticles, or 'teeth'. The thickened outer lips of many marine shells are often denticulate, sometimes along their entire length, as in helmet shells and cowries. Such a development is seldom seen in non-marine shells. Denticles are nearly always associated with thickened apertural lips, but in non-marine shells they may occur on lips of normal thickness. The edge of the aperture is in constant contact with the mollusc's mantle and so it is a natural place for it to deposit additional shelly material.

In lime-rich localities molluscs often secrete an excessive amount of calcium carbonate and this over-production may have a disastrous effect. The land-snail genus *Placostylus* contains several species of large size, some of which have heavy shells. All the species live on islands in the Pacific and in some places, such as New Caledonia, they are abundant. Several are dying out, however, because they have developed such thick and ponderous shells that they cannot move very far

A pair of Thorny Woodcocks (**Murex pecten**). *This well-known Pacific shell – also called the Venus Comb – has for long been a strong favourite with collectors.*

when they reach maturity. Most of the extra weight is apparently concentrated around and within the aperture.

Apertural denticles are particularly well developed in some tun shells, nearly all cowries and some whelks. The European Dog Whelk (*Nucella lapillus*) varies the appearance of its apertural teeth according to environmental factors, the production of strongly developed teeth being apparently correlated with food shortage. In some rock shells the presence of a single apertural tooth, which is relatively long and robust, indicates that the mollusc is carnivorous and uses the tooth to help force open the valves of bivalve shells.

It is among the carnivorous land snails, especially the small species from tropical countries, that the apertural armament is most pronounced. Some species belonging to the family Streptaxidae have their apertures so blocked up by tooth-like or lamellar processes that only a narrow chink is left through which the animal can squeeze in or out. In an unrelated land-snail genus (*Plectopylis*) there are barriers of shelly material placed well back in the aperture and these block the exit almost completely.

It is interesting to note that the only reliable way to identify species of *Plectopylis* is to break away the shell wall to reveal these barriers. Each species constructs them in different ways and in no two species do they seem to be identical. Such barriers allow the mollusc sufficient room for movement in and out of the aperture, but help to prevent the entry of predators such as insects. Although ants have been found caught in them it is possible that the barriers have a very different primary function. They may be simply devices for ensuring that the shell is carried in a position comfortable for the animal.

Another form of internal sculpture is found on the columella, the central pillar around which the shell-tube of a gastropod is coiled. In volutes, mitres and auger shells (among others) the columella is encircled by one or more folds. These give additional area for attachment muscles and enable the animal to move about without losing its shell. Some instances have been recorded of animals becoming detached from their shells, wandering about for a while and then returning to their shells again. This phenomenon has been recorded among winkles, cones and a very small number of non-marine molluscs.

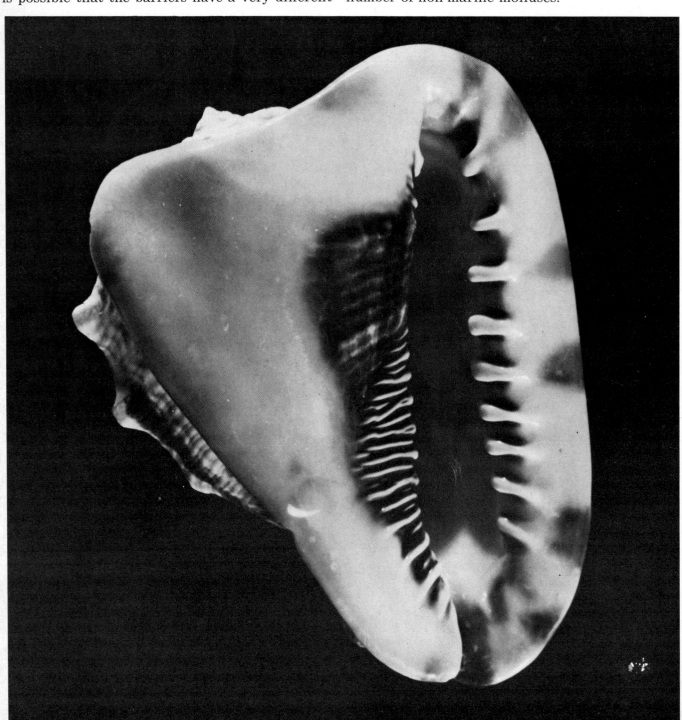

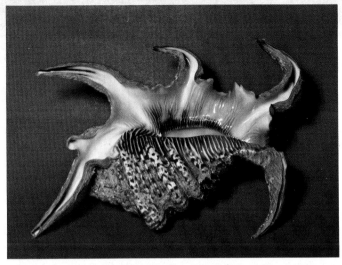

Opposite   The King Helmet (**Cassis tuberosa**)*, a large and heavy species found in the Caribbean*

Left   The Chiragra Spider Conch (**Lambis chiraga**)*, a common Pacific mollusc*

Below   The Many-Ribbed Harp (**Harpa costata**)*, one of the many outstanding species from Mauritius*

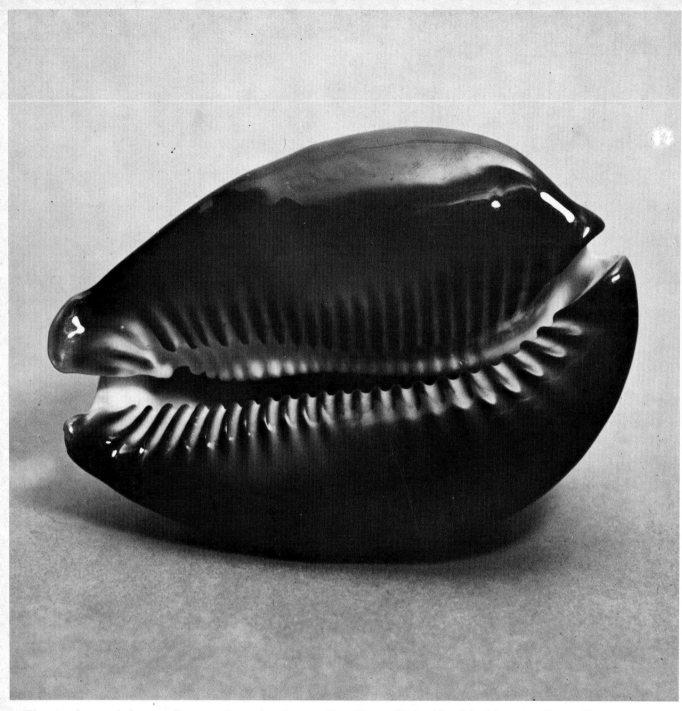

The sculptural forms discussed so far have all developed out of the substance of the hard shell and they are all more or less permanent features. There are also a few instances of sculpture being confined to the less permanent periostracum. Some shells are covered with a thick, fibrous periostracum and this may be extended into hair-like points or thin, plate-like processes (lamellae). Examples of a widely distributed frog shell, *Cymatium parthenopeum,* are represented in most museum collections by perfectly smooth shells, but they have a very different appearance in life. The fresh shell is shrouded in a thick, dark brown periostracum which is produced into long filaments rough to the touch. Many other frog shells are similarly, if less thickly, covered. Comparable periostracal coverings are found on ark shells

Above Underside of the Mauritian Cowry **(Cypraea mauritiana)** *showing the tooth-like processes surrounding the aperture*

Opposite A large hairy shell, **Trichotropis bicarinata,** *showing the periostracum flaking off*

(Arcidae) and bittersweet clams (*Glycymeris*). The Mossy Ark (*Arca imbricata*) has an almost shaggy, dark brown periostracum, whereas *Glycymeris glycymeris* has a thin velvety covering which rubs off easily. The hairy shells (*Trichotropis*) are cold-water species which develop prominent periostracal bristles unlike those on any other marine shells. The double row of bristles around its periphery suggested the name of the Two-keeled Hairy Shell (*Trichotropis bicarinata*).

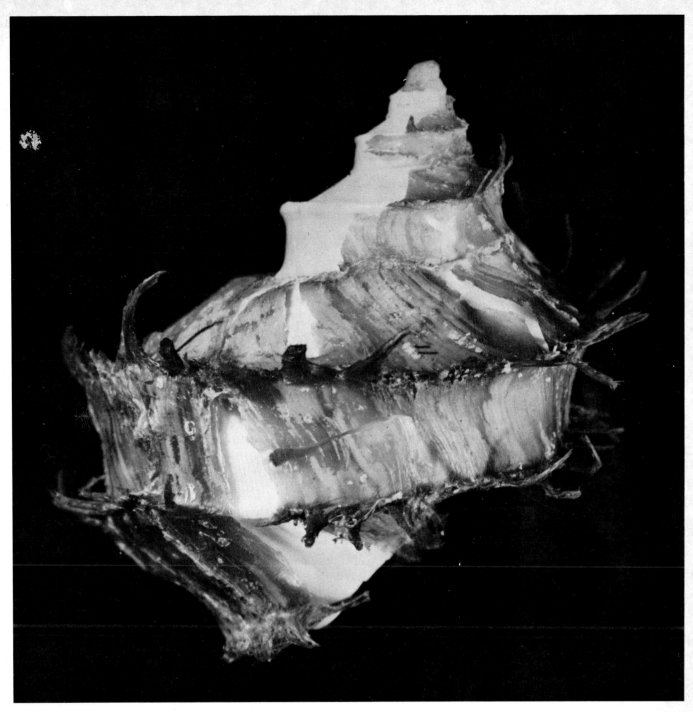

An approach to this type of periostracal growth is seen in a group of tropical land snails (Cyclophoridae). The shells of other land snails are covered with short bristles which, as in the Prickly Snail (*Acanthinula aculeata*) of European hedges and woods, trap particles of soil and leaf debris and so help them to acquire an effective camouflage. A few tropical land snails have a fringe of delicate, leaf-like filaments placed around the periphery of their shells.

A small New Zealand gastropod, *Potamopyrgus corolla*, is one of several small freshwater species having a few stiff bristles sticking out from the shell rather like the spines of a tiny sea urchin. The chitons are the only other kinds of molluscs which have spiny processes. In many species the surrounding girdle is more or less liberally decorated with tufts of bristles.

The geographical distribution of molluscs according to the degree of development of their spines has been little studied by specialists and, though presenting some points of interest, is less rewarding than a similar study of distribution according to colour and colour pattern. One or two generalizations are possible. The majority of gastropods and bivalves do not have spiny shells. Those which do are common in warm waters and the longest-spined shells are found in the warmest seas, such as those in which the Philippines and Borneo are situated. Most of them are found in shallow water but some live at considerable depths. Spiny non-marine molluscs are usually of small size and the spines are frequently restricted to the periostracal layer of the shell.

Shell Colour
and Pattern

In one respect it is difficult to discuss shell colour and colour pattern without mentioning shell sculpture. Many molluscs secrete the material which solidifies as sculptural features at the same time as they secrete pigments. Sculpture and pigments are thus amalgamated. For our purposes, however, it is preferable that these two products of molluscan secretory activity are studied separately. We need only remember that sculpture and pigment have a common origin (the mantle edge) and are usually associated intimately on or in the substance of the shell.

Most shells are coloured and many of them have evolved intricate and beautiful colour patterns. Often a single species will show great variation in colour and pattern, but it is more usual to find only a moderate amount of variation. Apart from their aesthetic appeal, colour and patterns help us to identify molluscan species. Without colour shells would be much less pleasing to the eye and would attract fewer students to the pursuit of conchology.

As the mantle secretes the substances which eventually harden to form solid shell it may also secrete different pigments, and these are distributed over the shell in various ways. Molluscs developed colour patterns on their shells many millions of years ago (in Ordovician times), as is evident from studies of fossils under ultraviolet light, and essentially the same kinds of patterns are found on the fossils as on modern specimens. It is reasonable to believe that colours and colour patterns on shells are of great importance to those molluscs which display them, but this belief is only partially borne out by the facts.

The biochemistry of shell pigmentation is too complex a subject to be dealt with here in detail, but certain points concerning coloration can be usefully discussed. Pigment is secreted at the mantle edge and, once incorporated into the shell or periostracum, it is not altered in any way by the animal. It is as permanent (and as lifeless) as the shell itself. Colours are not superficial in a molluscan shell, although they may sometimes be confined to the periostracum. In many instances the pigments are soluble in acid, but when they are incorporated into the conchiolin of the shell or the periostracum some pigments are not extractable by acid treatment because conchiolin is insoluble in acid.

The association of conchiolin and pigment seems to be of significance in an evolutionary sense because molluscs having shells with acid-soluble pigments all live in the sea and are relatively primitive creatures (such as top shells, bubble shells, pen shells and hammer oysters). Conversely, those shells whose pigments are bound up with conchiolin belong to much more advanced molluscs (such as volutes and cowries among marine molluscs, and many terrestrial and freshwater forms).

If several freshly-collected sea shells are inspected it will be seen that the periostracum, which is a prominent feature of several major groups, is dull, of one colour (monochromatic), and often opaque. Remove it and the vivid colours and colour patterns of the shells are revealed underneath. Unquestionably the pigments in these molluscs are firmly seated in the solid substance of the shell and removal of the periostracum serves only to enhance the shell's appearance. It is otherwise with many land snails which, in colour and colour pattern at least, are the equals in beauty of many sea shells. Some large land snails found in the Philippine Archipelago, South America and elsewhere in the warmer parts of the globe have richly coloured and exquisitely patterned shells. The site of coloration, however, is the periostracum (composed almost entirely of conchiolin). If the periostracum is removed with a stiff brush all the pattern and most of the colour is removed too, the underlying shell rarely displaying any kind of pattern or more than one uniform tint. To see such shells in all their beauty it is necessary to immerse them in water or to coat them lightly with a vegetable oil. This, incidentally, is also the best way to see the colour and colour patterns of sea shells.

If pigment of a single colour is secreted constantly by the mantle along its whole length the resultant coloration will be monochromatic. Many shells are monochromatic but still more numerous are the polychromatic (multicoloured) ones. In polychromatic shells the mantle secretes two or more different pigments and the different colours are frequently localized on the shell as bands. A gastropod shell will have bands spiralling around the whorls. In a bivalve they radiate from the umbones out to the edges of the valves. A glance at a tray of assorted shells will show that many do not conform to this simple kind of colour pattern. This is because the continual growth, represented by spiral colour (and sculptural) bands of gastropods and coloured (and sculptured) rays of bivalves, is interrupted by a discontinuous or rhythmic activity at the mantle edge. This discontinuity manifests itself in straight or zig-zag lines, loops, streaks, chevrons and triangular lines of colour (and, sculpturally, in varices, ribs, ridges, lamellae and grooves).

In its simplest form the interaction of the continuous and discontinuous types of secretion is seen in a gastropod shell having a single spiral band of colour crossed at intervals by a single streak of another colour. This is well exemplified in several land snails. Usually there is more than one spiral colour band in gastropods and more than one ray in bivalves. In marine gastropods there appears to be no prevalent number of spiral bands, although three or four basic ones are characteristic of many of them. Many land snails, particularly of the most highly evolved groups,

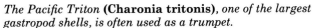
The Pacific Triton **(Charonia tritonis)**, *one of the largest gastropod shells, is often used as a trumpet.*

Kuroda's Volute **(Harpeola kurodai)**, *a recently discovered shell from Taiwan*

have five-banded shells, but it is rare to meet with more than five bands (although one or more of them may be subdivided to give a superficial appearance of a multi-banded type).

Some marine gastropods display many thin, spiral bands; others are only single-banded. Among bivalves the bands of colour radiating from the umbones vary so much in number and arrangement from species to species and group to group that no prevalent band number can be distinguished. Colour bands radiating from the umbones of freshwater bivalves are not commonly seen, although some freshwater mussels living in fast-flowing rivers have well-defined rays.

The bubble shells provide excellent examples of uninterrupted banding among gastropods, and comparable bivalve examples are found among the tellins. The majority of molluscs, however, have shells which show bands or rays more or less modified by the discontinuous activity of the mantle edge. In some the modifications are such

that it is extremely difficult to pick out even remnants of bands or rays. Sometimes transverse (or axial) streaks of colour are much more prominent than spiral bands or rays. This is well seen in Elliott's Volute (*Amoria elliotti*), in which the axial streaks are gently sinuous, and in its close ally, the Wavy Volute (*Amoria undulata*), in which they form a striking wavy pattern. In the Tent Olive (*Oliva porphyria*) the pattern is basically one of triangles; and *Lioconcha picta* is one of several bivalves having a very similar pattern.

Another interesting variation of axial colour pattern shows itself as a series of loops, such as are found between the ribs of harp shells, especially those of the Ventricose Harp (*Harpa major*). In this species the loops are dark compared with the rest of the shell and are united by points which are directed towards the edge of the aperture. By contrast, the similar loops on the shell of the Pacific Triton (*Charonia tritonis*) are directed away from the aperture.

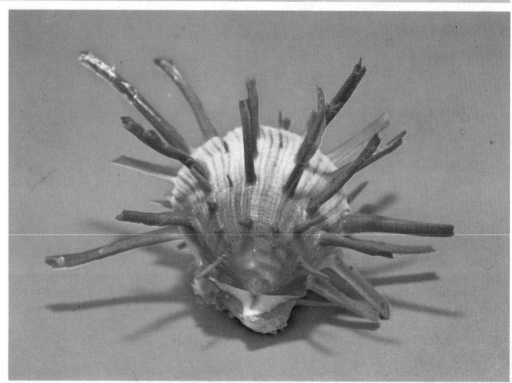

*Opposite above   Variation in common Philippine Islands
nerite,* **Neritina communis**

Opposite   Atlantic Thorny Oyster **(Spondylus americanus)**
from Florida and the Caribbean

Above   The Violet Snail **(Janthina janthina)** *and its egg
raft. This snail floats upside down at the surface of the sea.*

The spiral bands of gastropods and the rays of bivalves are sometimes broken up in a regular or irregular way to form rows of blobs, spots, dashes and dots. Such markings may cover the whole shell and so give it a chequered appearance. In rare instances the coloration will show right through the thickness of the shell and be more highly coloured on the inside than on the outside. Rings of colour are seen only very occasionally, but there are several examples among the cowries. The ringed pattern found on the Eyed Cowry (*Cypraea argus*) is particularly striking.

Like other colourful animals molluscs make use of some colours more than others. White is the colour most often encountered and is the background on which most of the others are displayed. Brown, red, pink, orange and yellow are often found either on their own or in combination with others. Violet is the predominant colour of underlying shell layers in such groups as the cowries. Blue and green are rarely encountered in marine shells. In non-marine shells, apart from the olivaceous hue of most freshwater shells, green is even rarer—the Green Tree Snail (*Papustyla pulcherrima*) is almost uniquely bright green— while blue is found in a mere handful of terrestrial species. Black is never found among shells but very dark colours are frequently encountered, especially very dense brown or brownish-purple.

The more sunshine they receive the more colourful shells are likely to be, but there are many exceptions. Those from deep water are usually white or pinkish in colour and may have a dull brownish periostracum. The most brilliantly coloured ones are those which inhabit the littoral zones or coral reefs of tropical regions, the colours

Above **Amusium japonicum,** *a large edible mollusc found in shallow water around Japan. The upper valve is reddish in colour and the lower valve is yellowish-white.*

Below   A very rare all-white specimen of a harp shell – probably the Heavy Harp **(Harpa crassa)** *from the Indian Ocean. This form was once considered to be a separate species* **Harpa virginalis.**

seeming to increase in brilliancy the nearer their habitats are to the equator.

Most bivalves have identical colour patterns on each valve but in a few species, such as *Amusium japonicum*, the upper valve is a rich dark colour and the lower one almost white. The reasons for this dissimilarity are not fully understood, although it is noteworthy that the lighter-coloured valve is the lower one and consequently less exposed to the light. An absence or a reduction of light affects the coloration of some molluscs living in shallow water or even out of it. Many marine gastropods having a flat or flattish base, such as *Tectum pyramis*, generally have a lighter colour on the base than on the spire. One of the rare exceptions is the shell of the Violet Snail (*Janthina janthina*), a species which floats on the surface of the sea. Significantly, it floats in such a way that its base is turned upwards towards the light.

The prevalence of dark-coloured, or melanistic, shells in some parts of the world has been often noticed, and it is a striking feature of a large number of shallow-water gastropods found along the entire western side of South America. On that rocky coast abound dark-coloured turban shells, top shells, limpets and chitons. The reason for this phenomenon may be the lowered temperature of the water, caused by the influence of the cold Humboldt Current which bathes the coast. This seems the more probable when a comparison is made between these shells and those found on the eastern side of South America. None of the latter shows such a markedly melanistic coloration. Cowries occasionally exhibit melanistic tendencies in very warm waters, particularly around New Caledonia and in the Red Sea.

The opposite phenomenon, albinism, is much commoner and more widespread among molluscs. Paradoxically, the higher frequency of albinism is due, in about equal measure, to a limitation of sunlight or to a superabundance of it. The white or whitish coloration of deep-sea molluscs and all those which are parasitic inside other creatures is the obvious result of an existence hidden from the light. In dry and arid parts of the world, on the other hand, land snails tend to have thick, white shells. The thickness insulates the animals from the sun's heat and the whiteness helps to reflect the heat away. Albinistic forms of normally coloured shells are known but the phenomenon is rarer among marine than non-marine molluscs. Land snails from northern and usually mountainous regions are often found with albinistic shells.

The colour of the shell is no sure guide to the colour of its tenant, and shell and animal may be of opposite coloration. The glossy white exterior of the Poached-Egg Cowry (*Ovula ovum*) contains a jet-black animal. The shells of some tropical volutes, having some of the most brilliantly coloured and exquisitely patterned shells in the world, are often outshone by those of the animals inside them. Some land snails have their shells partially or entirely translucent, so that the coloration of the animal shows through to the outside. Many molluscs have extremely thin and fragile shells with no colour at all.

The onlooker is constantly dazzled and bewildered by the beauty and complexity of shells, and particularly by their colour and colour pattern. Sooner or later he is tempted to speculate on the possible utility of colour and colour pattern to a mollusc. Of course all humans look at such things through eyes attuned to what pleases or satisfies them in one way or another. We find it almost impossible to believe that such lovely colours and designs are purposeless, and so we assume that there must be a reason for them. An immediate difficulty presents itself when we see that some of the most strikingly coloured and patterned shells are covered, in life, with a thick and to us, unsightly periostracum. That such exquisite decoration should be completely lost to view baffles us completely.

We are no longer able to share the opinion put forward by an eighteenth-century student of shells that the Almighty so covered them that we might have the pleasure of discovering their underlying beauties for ourselves. On the other hand no one since then has provided a satisfactory answer. Charles Darwin is only one of many students who failed to find any evidence of the employment by molluscs of colour and pattern as secondary sexual characteristics, the principal objection being their obliteration by the periostracum. Indeed, molluscs seem to have little or no regard for the beauty of each other's shells.

It is possible that there is a simple explanation for shell colour and pattern: shell growth and pigment secretion must react to form patterns of some kind, so why not the patterns we see? A gastropod and a bivalve can have similarly patterned shells and totally dissimilar habits. This is no more evidence that the similar pattern serves a similar purpose than that it serves no purpose at all. It is generally assumed that pigments represent waste products which have to be disposed of by the mollusc in some manner. Apparently they are disposed of by being incorporated into the shell or the periostracum.

It remains to be proved that molluscs can distinguish different colours and colour patterns. There are many molluscs which have survived very well without the benefit of beautiful colours on their shells. Nature is full of wonderful examples of symmetry, sculpture and pattern comparable to or exceeding the beauty of those to be found among molluscs. But it is human beings who pronounce these things beautiful. It is also a human characteristic to look for hidden meaning in all forms of beauty. Perhaps we should be content with the beauty and not meddle with the meaning.

Above   A group of strawberry shells **(Clanculus)** *from the Indo-Pacific region*

Right   Ventricose Harp **(Harpa major)**

Opposite   The Pacific Triton or Trumpet Shell **(Charonia tritonis)**

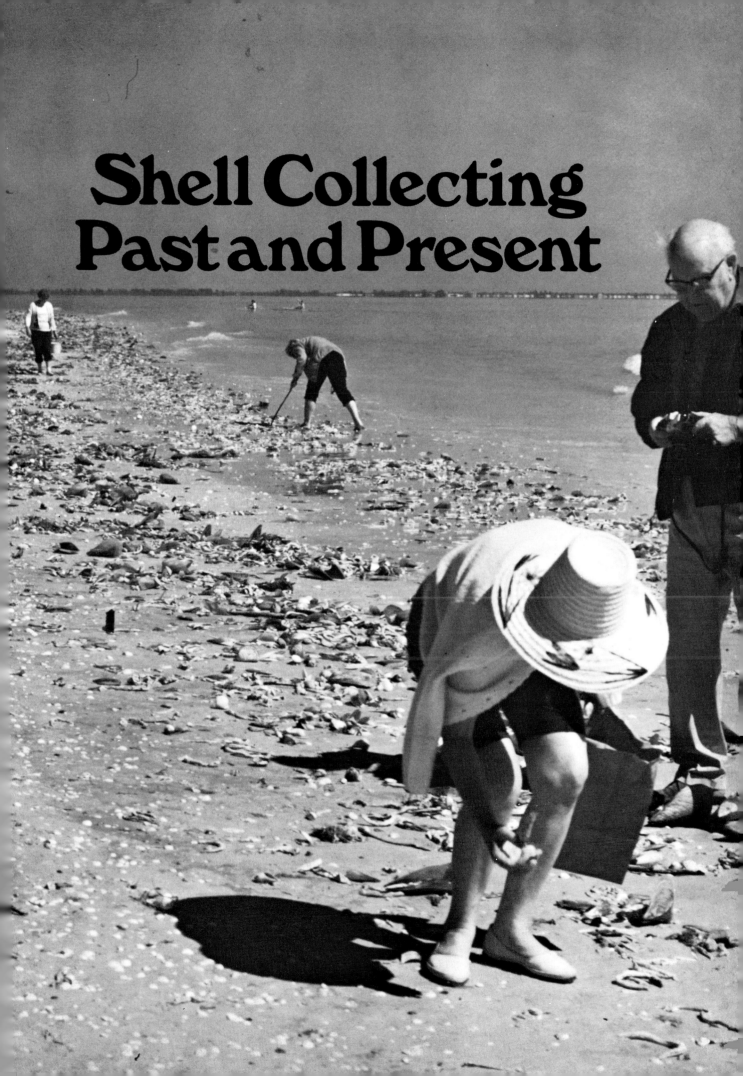

Shell Collecting
Past and Present

It is thought that in the fourth century B.C. Aristotle may have possessed a collection of shells and other natural objects for study, but we have no proof of this. Two centuries later, however, we are on surer ground. Laelius and Scipio, two celebrated Roman consuls, are known to have collected shells as a form of relaxation from official duties. In another chapter mention is made of a collection of exotic shells dug up out of the buried city of Pompeii. This is the first evidence we have of a collection of shells being accumulated for reasons other than that of personal adornment (although it is possible that their owner intended to decorate his house or garden with them).

About five centuries ago, during the Renaissance, wealthy patrons of the arts and sciences began to make collections of natural as well as artificial objects. Shells became important and expensive items in the 'cabinets of the curious', as they were called, and specimens worthless by modern standards were often valued as highly as works of art which are now considered priceless. Since it was easier at that time to acquire works of art than exotic natural objects the high prices given for shells are readily explained.

Because of its close and constant ties with the East Indies, Holland became a leading centre for the sale, purchase and appreciation of natural objects. Among these were seashells obtained at ports or trading stations in Java, Sumatra and elsewhere in the Malay Archipelago.

During the sixteenth and seventeenth centuries collections of natural objects were to be found in most of the leading cities in Europe. Even then several collectors specialized in shells, which also attracted the attention of painters and poets. Rembrandt and many lesser Dutch and Flemish artists painted them, poets eulogized them, Palissy the Huguenot potter moulded designs of them and scientists tried to classify them. Art and poetry were then in full flower but science, especially the science of living things, was still in its infancy.

It was a very long time before any books were published which added anything of significance to the writings of Aristotle. Few useful commentaries were written about molluscs, and the rare illustrations of shells were usually crudely engraved. The first book dealing exclusively with shells, the work of an Italian Jesuit called Buonanni, did not appear until 1681. It was followed, soon afterwards, by two incomparably better books, by the Englishman Lister and the German Rumphius respectively, but students and collectors still found it difficult to acquire more than a rudimentary knowledge of molluscs.

Just how small a part was played by science in those days is well shown by the way in which shells and other natural objects were arranged for display. The numerous paintings of 'cabinets of the curious', dating from the seventeenth century, reveal a complete lack of scientific arrangement. Shells, sharks' teeth, fish scales and seahorses shared the same table, box or shelf as statuettes, porcelain cups, coins and medals.

There was little improvement during the early years of the eighteenth century. Sometimes the collector would place some specimens under a glass dome or pyramid and surround them with bits of coral and seaweed. The desire to produce eye-catching set-pieces occasionally resulted in the formation of pleasing designs, but more often the results were ludicrous. By using wooden cut-out frames many Dutch collectors achieved interesting and easily modified arrangements of shells, which delighted dilettante observers but must have bewildered and disgusted those men whose interest in shells was more scientific.

Collectors sometimes allowed their imaginations full sway when arranging their shells and it is evident that pleasing arrangements meant more to them than the shells themselves. It was not unusual to find them made up into semblances of grotesque human figures. Even in the early eighteenth century such absurdities were still popular enough to be perpetuated in semi-scientific treatises, such as the *Thesaurus* of the Dutch apothecary Seba. In a large volume, devoted principally to shells, the reader's eye is arrested by a design, supposedly representing the contents and layout of one of Seba's cabinet drawers, displaying a fantastic arrangement of shells, the principal component of which is a satyr's head. But at least Seba's shells were kept in a cabinet and could be hidden away. Other collections, even more fantastic in arrangement, were perpetually on view. The king of Poland, Augustus II, stuck most of his shells on walls. One room in the royal residence had its walls covered with ornamental scrolls, grotesque masks, animal figures, bouquets of flowers and plates of fruit all made out of shells. It is only fair to add that the king also had a large collection of shells in glass-lined cabinets.

This deplorable attitude to natural history resulted, in part, from the lack of any consistent methods of classifying natural objects. There were no standard reference books to which everyone could look for guidance when they wished to arrange their collections, and so it was left to each collector to present things as he thought fit. The problem was made much worse by the lack of a uniform system of nomenclature. Animals and plants were known only by their popular names and these varied from country to country according to the language spoken.

Zoological and botanical nomenclature was eventually simplified through the untiring efforts of one man, Carl von Linné (better known as Linnaeus), one of the shining lights of Swedish science. By adopting a system which gave each

The Aulica Volute (Aulica aulica), *a fine, deep-red specimen*

Opposite   The Eyed Cowry **(Cypraea argus)**, *a favourite collector's item from the Indo-Pacific region*

Above   The white of the Poached-egg Cowry **(Ovula ovum)** *contrasts strikingly with the black of the animal's body*

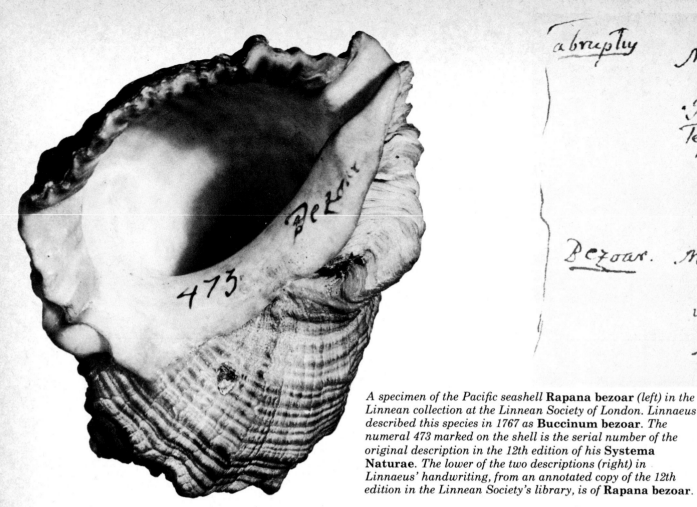

A specimen of the Pacific seashell **Rapana bezoar** *(left) in the Linnean collection at the Linnean Society of London. Linnaeus described this species in 1767 as* **Buccinum bezoar.** *The numeral 473 marked on the shell is the serial number of the original description in the 12th edition of his* **Systema Naturae.** *The lower of the two descriptions (right) in Linnaeus' handwriting, from an annotated copy of the 12th edition in the Linnean Society's library, is of* **Rapana bezoar.**

animal and plant a two-part, latinized name he enabled the classification and arrangement of natural objects to be approached in a logical and scientific way. The modern system of zoological nomenclature dates from 1758, the year in which Linnaeus published the tenth edition of his *Systema Naturae.* Proceeding from the assumption that a very large group of animals or plants can be subdivided into lesser groups, he gave each group (or genus) a collective (or group) name, known as a generic name. Each genus consisted of one or more species to which a species name was given. Henceforth a mollusc could be referred to by an unvarying two-part name. For example, the shell which is still referred to by some as the Commercial Trochus is correctly known by the name Linnaeus gave to it in 1758: *Trochus niloticus.* This is the name by which it is known in most shell books today. Without such a simple system of naming we should have to invent one or choose to call the shell by one of the numerous common names by which it was once known—'die glatte Pyramide' or 'der groste gefleckte Kräussel' in German; 'Marbled Top-shell' or 'Great Red-waved Top-shell' in English.

Shell collectors sometimes complain that latinized scientific names are too complicated. It is, however, indisputable that Linnaeus did everyone a great service when he introduced his simple nomenclatural scheme. With a system to work to and a simplified form of naming to follow, collec-

tors were able to give their collections a tidier, more professional appearance. By the end of the eighteenth century the more absurd arrangements of shells had disappeared.

To ensure a neat arrangement of shells it is imperative that they be prevented from rolling about. Linnaeus kept his shells in rectangular metal containers, but wooden boxes or partitioned drawers were easier to make and were favoured by collectors for many years, certainly until well into the present century. During the nineteenth century the unfortunate habit of glueing shells down on pieces of wood, card or glass came into vogue, particularly in some of the larger museums. Shells so mounted are disfigured by the glue, liable to be broken, and are notorious dust catchers. The practice can be condoned now only for exhibition purposes.

During the middle years of the nineteenth century some collectors favoured cabinet drawers lined with sheet cotton-wool on which they laid their specimens. A few collectors pasted a number of specimens of a species (usually three of each) onto a piece of tape and to one of the shells a small label was affixed. This ensured that the shells stayed with their labels but at the risk of defacing the shells.

Glass-topped boxes of various shapes and sizes came into use in the later nineteenth century and were standard equipment for collectors and museums for many years afterwards. They are now

...subecaudata perforata, spirae anfractibus sutura subexcava...
...tre tumido nodoso... carinato.
...in Tranquebaria. Sprengler.
...M. Spirillo / canaliculata... sed destituta cauda elongata
...ventre suo multo brevior, crassa, perforata. Anfractus
...riguntur summo margine spirae, sed ejus inferiori cin=
...in M. ... canaliculato, et tumidior evadit
perforata
...e caudata, anfractibus antice lamellis fluctu...
...tesp. 1. 18 J. G.
Tesdorp.
...magnitudine pomi, rudis, striata, postice subperforata.
...ventraly antice lamelly imbricaty exstantibus,
...aly more fluctuum aqua procellosa. Spira angulata
...by cylindricis, antice planiuscula rugosa. ventry ca...
...superior angulata fornicaty remy squamy la...
...exterius interre striatum

far too expensive to be widely used and their place has been taken by rectangular boxes made from clear plastic. Many collectors now have these receptacles, but they are not yet in general use in museums, where glass tubes and card trays have become standard equipment.

It is generally agreed among collectors that a data label, giving full information about the source of a specimen, is almost as important as the specimen itself. Indeed, unless an unlabelled shell is known to be that of an extremely rare species, or is of one known to inhabit a restricted locality, it is unlikely to be wanted by an advanced collector or by a museum. Even the commercial value of a shell is enhanced nowadays by its association with a fully documented label.

The earliest existing labels accompanying shells are in the Natural History Museum at Basle, Switzerland. They were written in the late sixteenth century, probably by Felix Platter, an anatomist and collector of natural curiosities who lived in Basle and died in 1614. Towards the end of the seventeenth century, however, the value of labelling and cataloguing specimens had been realized by several intelligent collectors. One of the men who lent specimens to Lister to be illustrated in his great shell book, the *Historia Conchyliorum*, was William Courten, whose collection of natural objects was widely recognized in his day as one of the most complete ever made. A small paper label recording the locality and other information was pasted onto each specimen and a catalogue number added.

Sir Hans Sloane, whose collection was the nucleus of that now housed in the British Museum, also catalogued his shells, but instead of pasting data labels on them he wrote a catalogue number directly on the shell. This was correlated with a catalogue which was kept with the collection (and which still exists). Because of Sloane's conscientious attitude to documentation some of his shells, clearly labelled or numbered, have been rediscovered in recent years. Since some of them are the original specimens illustrated in Lister's book, they have considerable historical interest as well as scientific value. Hugh Cuming dominated shell collecting during the early nineteenth century. By collection, exchange and purchase he built up a vast collection which was bought by the British Museum in 1866.

Unfortunately many later collectors neglected this aspect of collecting and, because of their negligence, many thousands of shells of scientific value have been lost sight of. Even during the nineteenth century, when most collectors were aware of the value of documentation, some of them were strangely lax in their attitude to labels. John Dennison of Liverpool possessed a collection which was the envy of other enthusiasts. He had plenty of money and leisure and used both to build up a large stock of rare shells. Despite the splendour of his cabinet, a magnificent rosewood affair

An illustration from Seba's **Thesaurus** *showing an arrangement of shells around a satyr's head*

*Linnaeus, the eighteenth century biologist who simplified the
nomenclature of animals and plants*

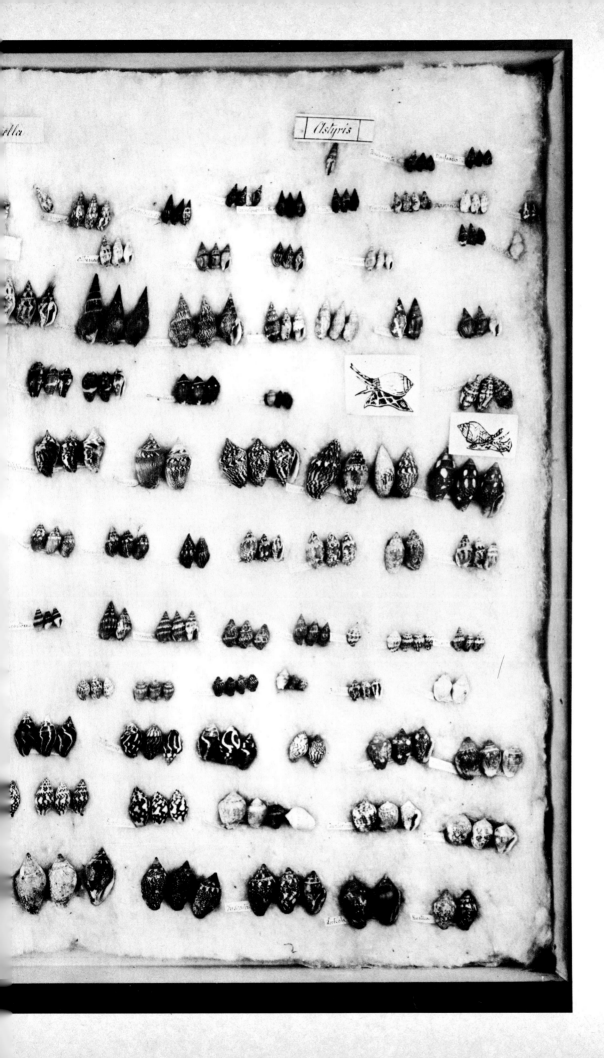

Previous pages   A Victorian shell collector's drawer. The shells are stuck onto strips of tape and labelled with the specific name. The cotton wool on which they are laid out is to keep the shells in place.

Opposite   A large collection in all sizes of the Paper Nautilus **(Argonauta argo)**

Below   A drawer from the Banks collection

J. Faber fecit 1729

D^nus Hans Sloane Baronettus

Collegij Regij Medicorum Londinensiū & Regiæ Societatis Præses &c.

13

Printed for Bowles & Carver, N°69 in St Pauls Church Yard. London.

Opposite Sir Hans Sloane (1660–1753)

Above Hugh Cuming (1791–1865) accumulated the largest and most valuable collection of all time.

Below Shells from the Sloane collection. All of them are the actual specimens illustrated by Martin Lister in his **Historia Conchyliorum**.

decorated with painted panels, the shells were thrown carelessly into the drawers without labels or information of any kind. Ironically, the sale of his collection in 1865 was a great event and attracted the attention of many collectors and expert conchologists.

Before shells can be labelled and arranged they have to be cleaned and identified. Many artifices have been employed to show off shells to best advantage. From the time of the Renaissance to the early nineteenth century it was not considered sufficient merely to remove the animal from its shell (which is the only aspect of cleaning which is absolutely essential if a shell is to be preserved in a dry state). For many early collectors cleaning implied removing anything which did not please the eye of the beholder, and this sometimes meant removing a lot more than the animal (which would usually have been extracted anyway before the shell came into the possession of the dealer or the collector).

As the chapter on freaks and frauds shows, in the hands of eighteenth-century Dutch and French dealers and their employees, the art of shell cleaning became the art of shell adulteration. At that time the pearly gleam of a shell's underlying layers constituted one of its most compelling features, and so it was scraped, rubbed and polished until all, or nearly all, of its surface was smoothed down and its natural excrescences obliterated. One reason for this practice was a shortage of different kinds of shells having collector-appeal, a shortage which ended in the nineteenth century as more and more new and attractive shells were brought into Europe. The conchological treasures of New Zealand, Australia, the Philippines and Polynesia were pleasing enough in their natural state for over-zealous cleaning to become superfluous.

Today collectors are usually content to clean out the animals and brush away the marine growths adhering to the shell. Since marine growths, particularly incrustations of coral, can be unsightly and cannot be removed effectively by merely brushing, some collectors plunge incrusted shells into a weak bleaching solution to soften up and help dislodge the growths. These are then fairly easy to brush off, persistent adhesions being chipped away with a knife or similar instrument. There is still a demand for shells which have been rubbed down and highly polished, however, and since they may be sold for considerably more than if they remained in their natural state, there are many of them on the market.

It is only since the end of the Second World War that collectors have acquired most of their shells by their own exertions or by exchange with other collectors. Before then they relied heavily on dealers to supply them with specimens, especially the more attractive shells from tropical regions. The procedure by which a shell was translated

Above   The Precious Wentletrap **(Epitonium scalare)**, *formerly the most coveted of all seashells*

Right   The Spotted Cowry **(Cypraea guttata)**, *a very rare species from the south-west Pacific*

Opposite above   The Paper Nautilus **(Argonauta argo)**. *This exceedingly fragile object is not a shell but an egg case.*

Opposite below   The Golden Cowry **(Cypraea aurantium)**, *the most coveted of all cowries*

from its natural habitat to the collector's cabinet was fairly standard. As Europeans opened up different parts of the world to exploration and commerce, some of the novel objects encountered by sailors and others were stowed away in ships homeward bound for ports in Holland, France, England and elsewhere in Europe. Among those objects were bags of shells picked up on distant beaches and reefs or acquired by exchange with natives. Some of these were kept by their owners but most of them were for sale. Those bought by the dealers were sold later at greatly increased prices.

For many years the West Indies, the Indian Ocean and the East Indies were the sources of most of the exotic shells seen in Europe. Then, following the opening up of the Pacific Ocean by Captain James Cook and others, that ocean became a primary source of shells. The way was now open for explorers, adventurers and paid collectors to investigate previously unworked coasts. Paid collectors were those men and women who were prepared to risk their lives to enrich the collections of wealthy patrons.

Such men and women brought to the attention of collectors and scientists hundreds of new species of molluscs, many of which have not been collected since. The Victorian era was the heyday of these courageous and enterprising people, and our knowledge of most of the world's exotic land and freshwater shells, largely neglected and unknown before they came on the scene, was greatly enriched by their endeavours.

Some probed the sea bed for new shells. One or two used their own yachts or hired vessels suitable for dredging in fairly deep water. Most of them risked their lives in tiny boats to do the same thing. But bravery and small boats were inadequate resources with which to explore the abyssal depths of the oceans. At depths which can be measured in miles well-equipped ocean-going vessels are essential for this kind of work.

Oceanographical exploration came of age with the voyage of H.M.S. *Challenger* in the 1870s. Other ships, such as the *Albatross* from the United States and the *Travailleur* from France, continued the exploration of the sea floor. There are ships on the high seas now whose main task it is to find out what lives at depths where light never penetrates and where water pressure would reduce a human being to pulp. Down there are some of the world's most remarkable shells, few of which ever reach a collector's cabinet.

Perhaps the most remarkable single fact to have emerged from deep-sea research is the discovery of living animals and plants in the deepest parts of the sea. Living molluscs have been brought up from depths of more than five miles. Many more molluscs are certainly awaiting discovery by research vessels, but it is doubtful if the entire deep-sea mollusc fauna of the world's oceans will approach anywhere near the quantity and variety of the shallow-water fauna. The richest place for molluscs is the continental shelf bordering a land mass, particularly in the tropics. The littoral zone, lying between high-tide and low-tide marks, is especially favoured by warmth-loving molluscs.

Although a great many shells in good condition may be collected in the littoral zone, the best of them are found at depths just beyond our reach. Popular handbooks insist that the only time when certain molluscs may be found by paddlers on the shore is at the extreme low water of spring tides. This means that only for a few days in the year, not all of them in the warmest season, is it possible to do really effective collecting. Unless dredging is done from a boat, collecting is usually limited to what can be found between tide-marks. Fortunately, the problems of collecting have now been minimized by the advent of a remarkable piece of equipment: the aqualung.

A well-known American collector and authority on molluscs has written: 'The aqualung has done for shell collecting what the cotton gin did for the South, what the assembly line did for the automobile, what the mechanical reaper did for the farmer. In short it has revolutionized the hobby'. Perfected by Commander Jacques Yves-Cousteau during the Second World War, this apparatus allows the swimmer to move around freely under water with his air supply strapped on his back. With it divers have descended to more than 350 feet (and many shell collectors habitually descend to half that depth in their search for specimens).

The present popularity of shell collecting as a hobby is due in large part to the widespread use of the aqualung: places that were once considered impregnable are being investigated thoroughly. The interstices of coral reefs, underwater caves, sunken wrecks, and other rewarding habitats which cannot be sampled by the dredge are now the stamping grounds of collectors just as much as the littoral zone.

Some of the shells which are offered for sale nowadays have been collected at great personal risk. The dangers which the underwater searcher may encounter include fierce eels, venomous water snakes, sharks, stinging jellyfish, razor-sharp corals, and perhaps most deadly of all, the 'bends', that agonizing and crippling illness which results from bubbles of nitrogen being released into the blood stream when the swimmer ascends too rapidly from a considerable depth. Air embolism can also cripple or kill and occurs under the same conditions—the trapped, compressed air in the lungs is forced, because of decreasing external pressure, into the blood stream from the lungs. This should be remembered when a beautiful shell comes up for sale at one of the world's leading auction houses or is advertised by a dealer. The winning bid at auction or the dealer's asking price may seem inordinately high to those whose shell collecting is done at second hand but the person who collected it may have flirted with death and suffered pain in the attempt.

The pleasures of shell collecting are many and varied, and men and women from all walks of life are succumbing to its charms in increasing numbers. All derive a lasting pleasure from what is now a very popular pastime. Shell clubs are being formed in many countries, and journals and books for popular guidance are being published in several languages. Shell collecting, it seems, is here to stay. But is it reasonable and sensible to collect living molluscs?

Some species, important as food, are harvested in millions annually, but their collecting is usually controlled. Those species collected as cabinet specimens are in a different category. To collect empty shells from the beach is harmless: they would soon disintegrate anyway. To collect living specimens may also be harmless if the species are abundantly represented or are pests of commercially exploited molluscs. Others may be so scarce that to collect one living specimen could affect the continued survival of the species. In practice this applies to a few living molluscs having a very restricted range, such as land shells on oceanic islands. It is rarely true of marine molluscs.

In many parts of the world living molluscs washed up on a beach by strong tides or storms are doomed. They cannot get back to their offshore habitat, and will be rolled or crushed to death. These molluscs may be collected without altering the balance of nature at all. Collecting two or three living specimens from a greater number is also reasonable providing too many collectors are not combing a restricted area. To collect immature specimens of rare species is unreasonable because they have not been allowed to reproduce their own kind. With some notable exceptions, however, it is unlikely that the supply of molluscs in the world's seas is diminishing mainly because they are being hunted by collectors of specimens.

Large commercial concerns are more deserving of blame. The curio trade, carried on briskly in many parts of the world, is responsible for the stockpiling of shells for dispatch to factories where they will be cut up, shaped, polished and painted to satisfy the ephemeral interests of tourists and holidaymakers. A large shell factory measures its intake of specimens by the ton. The weight and volume of shells passing through such an establishment in a year exceeds by far the total weight and volume of shells which pass through the hands of all the world's specimen-shell collectors over a similar period.

The use of explosives as a means of stunning and catching fish has disastrous effects on coral reefs in the tropics, and molluscan life suffers badly in consequence. Moreover, the devastating results of spilt crude oil on all forms of coastal life are witnessed only too often to be dismissed as trivial.

On land the felling of ancient forests to make way for more profitable timber trees or for valuable building land exterminates populations of snails and other animals which cannot go and live elsewhere. The pollution of water supplies by industrial and shipping concerns, with the consequent destruction of animals and plants, is another familiar feature of present-day life. By the time these destructive agencies are rendered harmless there may be no molluscs and other defenceless forms of life left for us to observe and collect.

While this large-scale destruction is going on shell enthusiasts are continuing to collect the objects which give them so much pleasure. But should they be allowed to do so unchecked? It is claimed by some that the world's molluscan populations will suffer severely if their human predators are given free rein and, in a local sense, this is often true. It is said that a number of once familiar species are no longer available around Sanibel Island off the coast of Florida (that Mecca of the shell collector), where it is almost unknown for a beach to be without at least one collector at any time of day or night in the cool season.

Well-combed collecting areas in the United States, Australia, New Zealand and elsewhere are being denuded of their larger molluscs and indiscriminate collecting is apparently to blame for this. There is much surer evidence that some non-marine molluscs have been exterminated or populations of them decimated by the activities of greedy or unthinking collectors. Soon there may be no Green Tree Snails on Manus Island in the Pacific, simply because collector-demand is so high and the snails so easily obtained. They are exported by the sackful and must inevitably become extinct if preventive measures are not taken soon. The overall picture, however, indicates no massive depletion of stocks by shell collectors. There are still too many unfrequented localities to make this likely.

In some places laws have been passed forbidding or restricting the collecting of living molluscs in certain ways and at certain times. Since shell collecting is an advertised tourist attraction at some of the places where these laws have been passed, they are seldom, if ever, enforced.

It should be recognized, nevertheless, that shell collecting may have a very useful part to play in modern society as an occupation with considerable therapeutic qualities. Ever since Laelius and Scipio took up shell collecting as a means of relaxation it has given pleasure and peace to those who are troubled, tired or frustrated. The celebrated novelist George Eliot, who was a keen student of seashore life, was probably thinking of the pleasure she had derived from shell collecting when she wrote in *Middlemarch:* 'Why, you might take to some light study; conchology now; I always think that must be a light study'.

Freaks and Frauds

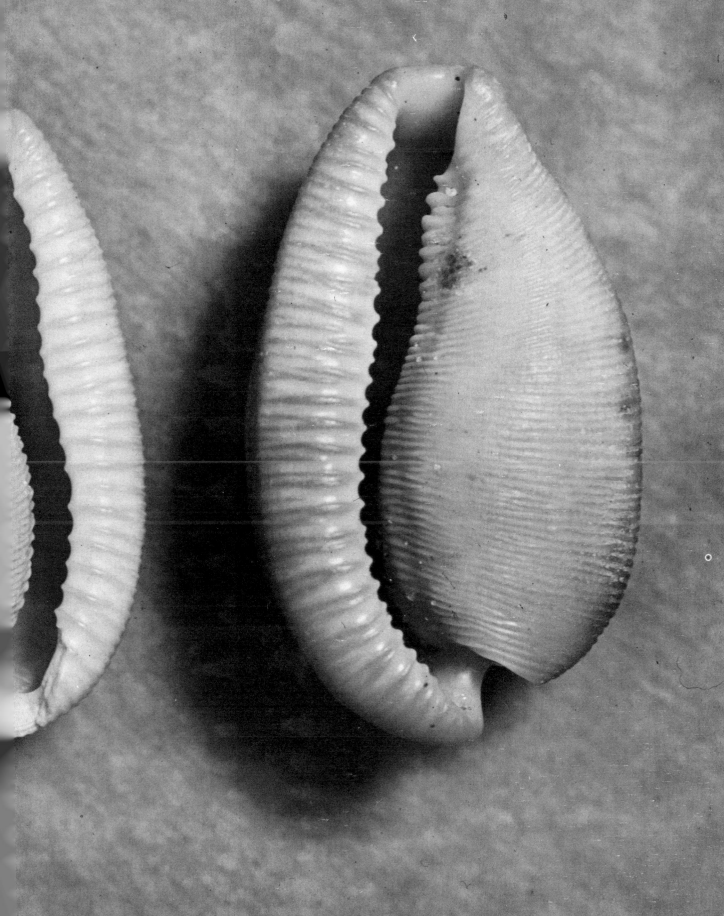

In most animal groups, from the lowliest to the most advanced, there occur specimens whose appearance is abnormal in one way or another. Sometimes the abnormality is so slight that it may be missed at first glance and apparently troubles the creature little or not at all. Other abnormalities are so extraordinary that they are not easily passed over and present obstacles to the creature's enjoyment of its normal way of life. Such abnormalities, distortions or monstrosities, as they are variously called, are often encountered among molluscs. They may affect either the shell or the animal's soft parts and occasionally both.

Among the abnormalities of the soft parts those most often recorded are: duplication or reduction of tentacles or other appendages of gastropods; the presence of three siphons or one (in place of two) in bivalves; and the development of extra tentacles in squids and octopuses. Among gastropods two eyes have been found on one tentacle, two tentacles and two eyes on one side of the head, and two heads on one body. A slit limpet was once found with two eyes on each side of its head, and slugs without any tentacles have been seen. Many other variations of the soft parts have been recorded, including abnormal forms of internal organs.

The operculum may be abnormal in certain species, and living specimens of molluscs which are normally operculated are often found without a trace of an operculum. Specimens of the Common European Whelk (*Buccinum undatum*), which is subject to so much abnormal variation, have been found bearing two opercula, and a similar duplication is known for the European Dog Whelk (*Nucella lapillus*). A specimen of the Common European Whelk supposedly found with three opercula was recorded by a distinguished British conchologist, J.G.Jeffreys, in the mid-nineteenth century. Apparently, a wealthy collector, John Leckenby of Scarborough, had got in touch with a number of whelk sellers and asked them to put aside any whelk so endowed. He also offered a generous reward. A specimen answering to the description was soon forthcoming and was successfully palmed off to a dealer acting for Leckenby. But Leckenby quickly saw that the shell with three opercula was a counterfeit and declined to purchase it. No specimen has ever been found with three naturally acquired opercula.

The most striking and bizarre abnormalities of molluscan morphology, however, are those which afflict the shell alone and it is to these that we will confine ourselves for the rest of this chapter. Before doing so it is interesting to note that a number of gastropods normally provided with shells have been seen crawling about without shells at all. A species of cone has been observed to leave its shell for a time and to return to it. Pond snails (*Lymnaea*) and winkles (*Littorina*) have been seen to do likewise.

With the possible exception of tusk shells and the primitive deep-sea monoplacophorans (*Neopilina*), every class of the Mollusca containing shell-bearing animals has produced numerous examples of abnormally formed shells. It must not be thought, however, that such abnormalities are common. Many are extremely rare.

The monstrous shells which are prized most of all by collectors are those in which the normal direction of coiling is reversed. The subject of reverse coiling in gastropods is of perennial interest to shell-collectors and others and is worth some discussion here.

In chapter 3 the coiling of gastropod shells was mentioned, but little attention was paid to the direction of coiling. Viewed from above the apex, most gastropods turn in a clockwise (or right-handed) direction. The shells of a number of non-marine snails turn in an anti-clockwise direction, and a few land snails have shells which turn either way indiscriminately. Very few marine gastropods have shells which normally coil in an anti-clockwise direction and only one family (Triphoridae) has a majority of species which do so. The direction of coiling of most gastropod shells is just one of the many proofs that we live in a 'right-handed' universe. Certainly, our world seems to have been made for right-handed organisms. A shell with normally clockwise, or right-handed coiling is said to be dextral. The opposite, or left-handed direction of coiling, is called sinistral.

A practised shell-collector will spot an abnormally sinistral shell immediately. Since such shells are extremely rare, they are naturally prized more highly than their normally coiled counterparts. In some species reverse coiling is relatively frequent, though it is not really common in any species, and a collector may go through life without owning one. Sinistral specimens of the Common European Whelk (*Buccinum undatum*) are rare and often the finder has been associated with the whelk industry all his life without ever seeing a similar specimen before. Frequently such discoveries are reported in the popular press and spark off columns of correspondence; they have never yet brought the pecuniary rewards so confidently expected by the discoverers. The truth is that sinistral specimens of the Common European Whelk can be found in many collections.

It is not the same with some other equally abundant species. Countless millions of the Common European Periwinkle (*Littorina littorea*) have been collected and consumed by humans, but probably less than a dozen reversed specimens are known today. The European Dog Whelk (*Nucella lapillus*) is abundant and conspicious enough around the coasts of Britain and France. Hundreds may be collected from a few square metres of rock in an hour or two, but it is doubtful if more than half a dozen reversed specimens have been recognized during the last two hundred years.

During the nineteenth century John Leckenby became well known for his infatuation with abnormal shells. On one occasion he offered ten pounds for a sinistral European Dog Whelk and induced a squad of Scarborough women to collect thousands of specimens for him, offering them so much per pint measure. Many bushels of shells were collected but to no avail, and so the squad was disbanded. Leckenby did not know that two of the women, less scrupulous and probably more intelligent than the others, brought the same shells for inspection over and over again.

One of the known sinistral specimens was actually found at Scarborough many years before this incident. It came into the hands of William Bean, a Scarborough shell-collector, in a curious manner. He had sent his grand-daughter to the pier on an errand, and when she returned he scolded her for having loitered on the way. She had been picking up shells by the pier and some of them fell to the ground as she was wiping the tears from her eyes with her pinafore. Bean was amazed and delighted to see that one of the shells was a sinistral European Dog Whelk and no doubt he forgave his grand-daughter immediately. Event-

Two shells of the Common European Whelk showing normal, dextral coiling (left) and abnormal, sinistral coiling (right). The illustration on the previous pages shows an extremely rare abnormality – a sinistral cowry – between two normal shells.

ually Bean also acquired a sinistral shell of the Common European Periwinkle, probably making him the only person who has ever owned both these rare monstrosities at one time.

The phenomenon of reverse coiling in marine gastropods is so unusual that it has been recorded in only about sixty species throughout the world. Margin shells (*Marginella*) comprise more than a third of this total, and no other marine genus includes more than four or five species which have produced sinistral monstrosities. It is strange that such a large proportion of sinistral marine gastropods should belong to a particular genus. Margin shells are certainly numerous in species and sometimes astonishingly abundant in specimens, but this could be said of several marine groups. The cones, for instance, comprise several hundred different species, and in some places cones are extremely common. But it was not until 1920 that a sinistral living cone was reported and, at the time of writing, only three living species are known to have produced sinistral shells.

The most desirable of all sinistral monstrosities is that of the Indian Chank (*Turbinella pyrum*) which, as mentioned in the chapter on shells and man, is highly prized and sometimes revered by those of the Hindu faith. Only about one in 6,250,000 is reversed and probably fewer than 300 have ever been found. Undoubtedly such a rare object would have been jealously guarded in an Indian household if one could have been obtained.

There are not many records of abnormally sinistral freshwater gastropods. Only in a group of pond snails (*Lymnaea*) can reverse coiling be considered at all common and only single specimens are recorded of most species in which this abnormality is known to occur. It is a very different picture with terrestrial snails. There are probably 200 or more species of which abnormally sinistral shells are known. Some produce these monstrosities rather frequently, such as the Roman Snail or Escargot (*Helix pomatia*), one of the largest and best-known of the edible snails of Europe. It has been estimated that in the vicinity of Geneva six out of every 18,000 specimens are sinistral. Very few dextral monstrosities of normally sinistral species are known, presumably because many fewer species are normally sinistral anyway.

Many explanations have been advanced to account for the phenomenon of reversed coiling in shells, but there is still no satisfactory answer. It used to be thought that an 'electric force' or injury at an early stage of growth was responsible. Nowadays biologists believe that the phenomenon begins at the egg stage, but they are still not sure what happens to the egg or why. Reversal seems to be much commoner in warm places and is unknown among molluscs which live under very cold conditions. It is noteworthy that some of the more remarkable monstrosities among molluscs originate in the warmer parts of the globe, but this does not prove that their monstrous appearance is due primarily to increased temperatures.

Many other things can happen to a shell to alter its appearance. Tall-spired shells may be distorted in such a way that the spire tends to lean to one side. The siphonal canals of such gastropods may also be distorted, and occasionally a shell is found with two canals in place of one. Shells of many gastropods have been reported in which the whorls are 'stepped' instead of being almost smooth-sided. Such monstrosities are said to be 'scalariform'. In a few species the process goes a stage further and the whorls appear to be completely unwound. In this condition they resemble the classical horn of plenty or cornucopia. These monstrosities are very rare and the known examples are nearly all referable to the Common Garden Snail (*Helix aspersa*) or the Escargot.

Sometimes a spire fails to develop normally and the shell is flat-topped. A competent conchologist once described a large swamp snail (*Pila*) as new to science because of this peculiarity, but it was merely an abnormal specimen of a well-known species. As recently as 1949 a specimen of the common Queen Conch (*Strombus gigas*), collected in the Bahamas, was described as a new species. The shell, of which several similar specimens are known, had a malformed body whorl and spire caused, presumably, by an imperfectly functioning mantle.

Some of the strangest monstrosities are to be found among the cowries. The most remarkable of these, in which there is a lengthening of the shell at the anterior and posterior extremities, are known as rostrate cowries. Such distorted cowries are often very dark in colour compared with normal ones, and they are frequently almost black or melanistic.

For many years it was thought that all rostrate and melanistic cowries originated in the waters around New Caledonia in the Pacific Ocean, but they are now known to live around Mauritius, on the Queensland coast of Australia and elsewhere. There is still no agreement about the causes of these monstrosities. They have been attributed to a disease of the cowry's mantle, to the effects of an internal parasite, to conditions of life on a muddy sea floor, and to excessive mineral content of the water. Such shells are highly prized by cowry collectors.

The number and arrangement of spines may vary considerably among specimens of a single species, and occasionally specimens are found with many more spines than normal or none at all. Scorpion shells (*Lambis*) have been recorded with more or less than the normal complement of 'fingers' at the edge of the outer lip, and sometimes the fingers are almost painfully deformed. Smooth-shelled species, such as cones and olives, never develop spines, but they are occasionally found with a raised band encircling the body whorl.

Abalones have produced some interesting anomalies of shell growth. Usually they develop a shell with a single row of holes, the earlier ones being filled in as growth proceeds, leaving open those formed last (less than half a dozen as a rule). It is rare to find mature abalone shells which depart from this arrangement, but there are a few notable exceptions. In the Channel Islands several Sea Ears (*Haliotis tuberculata*) have been found without any open holes at all. A similar absence of holes has been observed in the Black Abalone (*Haliotis cracherodei*) of the Californian coast.

The opposite abnormality has been noticed in the large White Ear Shell (*Haliotis laevigata*) of South Australia. Several were found at the same time in which all the holes were interconnected by a slit. More remarkable than these, however, is the record of a Giant Ear Shell (*Haliotis gigantea*) from Japan which had two rows of perforations instead of one. These abnormalities were not obviously detrimental to the full development of the molluscs whose shells they graced, but they were certainly not of obvious advantage to them either.

Of the many other naturally formed monstrosities it is worth mentioning gastropods having a double aperture. This abnormality has been noticed in numerous small land snails but is uncommon among seashells. Among bivalves monstrosities are less spectacular. Their valves may be distorted into various shapes by external circumstances, such as being wedged inescapably between immovable rocks. Occasionally one valve of a normally convex bivalve will be flatter than its partner, and sometimes a bivalve can develop a double shell, one within the other. The 'teeth' on the inside edges of some bivalves can be reversed

Natural and polished valves of the mussel **Choromytilus chorus**

partially or entirely, so that those proper to one valve appear in the opposite valve, and vice versa.

A curious abnormality noticed among chitons is the occasional reduction of the number of valves. A normal chiton has eight valves, but specimens have been found with seven, six, five or even three. There is, however, no record of a chiton having more than eight valves.

Mention has already been made of a fake whelk with three opercula as an example of a man-made monstrosity. There are other instances of shells which have been manipulated by human hands so that their appearance is altered. This practice was started in the early days of shell collecting when it was considered essential that shells intended for display should be thoroughly cleaned. During the seventeenth century it was customary to soak shells successively in salt water and fresh water, to dry them in the sun and then to rub them hard with a woollen cloth till they shone like glass.

In the following century shell cleaning became a recognized trade, and many artifices were employed to improve on the appearance, and consequently the commercial value, of sub-standard or common shells. Broken spines and missing apical whorls were cleverly replaced, apertural lips were filed smooth, unpaired valves of rare bivalves were married together, cracks and holes were filled in, faded colours were brightened up with paint, and worn or dull surfaces were coated with varnish. Papier-mâché was often used to replace missing pieces of shell. The Chinese used to make excellent facsimiles of the Precious Wentletrap with rice paste.

In eighteenth-century Holland and France the adulteration of shells for commercial gain was carried to excess. Many of the prized specimens seen in the cabinets of wealthy collectors before 1800 were partially or entirely fabricated and the fabrications had usually been passed off as rare and valuable specimens. The White Hammer Oyster (*Malleus albus*) of the Pacific Ocean was so rare then that dealers could not obtain sufficient specimens for their customers. Those which they did supply included some which had not been fashioned by nature. Another forgery, called the 'Golden Limpet', was distributed to collectors in Paris about 1767 as a new and strikingly attractive species. It was really a common species of limpet which had been brought from the Falkland Islands in some quantity. Its original reddish-brown coloration had been transformed into a brilliant gold after the shell had been gently fired in a pan or heated in hot cinders.

The application of heat may have a marked and permanent effect on shells of various kinds. The brown coloration of some shells may become white if touched with a hot iron. Many years ago a large volute bearing a series of conspicuous white spots was displayed in the National Museum of Natural History in Paris. In the 1780s a specimen of the common Lurid Cowry (*Cypraea lurida*), which had been given two rows of spurious spots by artificial means, was passed off as a new species at a Paris auction.

The effect of heat on some shells suggests that the described colour varieties of certain species are due entirely to its agency. One or two species of olives (*Oliva*) are very susceptible to heat treatment and, if held in a naked flame, will often turn a most attractive pink. Presumably the effect is much the same as if the shells had lain for a long time exposed to the heat of a tropical sun.

Another way to alter the coloration of a shell is to rub away the surface layer to reveal the differently coloured layer underneath. The purplish-violet hue of many worn shells is usually the result of natural weathering, but it has sometimes been imitated successfully by artificial means. The great eighteenth-century naturalist, Carl Linnaeus, described a cowry under the suggestive name of *Cypraea amethystea*. The shell on which his description is based is actually a rubbed down specimen of a species he had already described under another name. Tourists visiting Fiji are offered specimens of a shell known locally as the 'Tapa Cowry'. They are buying at a high price rubbed down specimens of the Humpback Cowry (*Cypraea mauritiana*), a common species in the Pacific Ocean.

About the middle of the nineteenth century monstrous shells of a very different kind were manufactured by French conchologists. Using the Common Garden Snail as their raw material, they carefully broke away the shell from the animal of an immature specimen and then introduced the still-living animal into a shell of similar size, but belonging to a species of dissimilar appearance. After a few days the animal attached itself by the columellar muscle to the new shell and eventually soldered the new growth of shell to the old. These man-made monstrosities were manufactured primarily for scientific purposes, although some of them were eventually sold at auction.

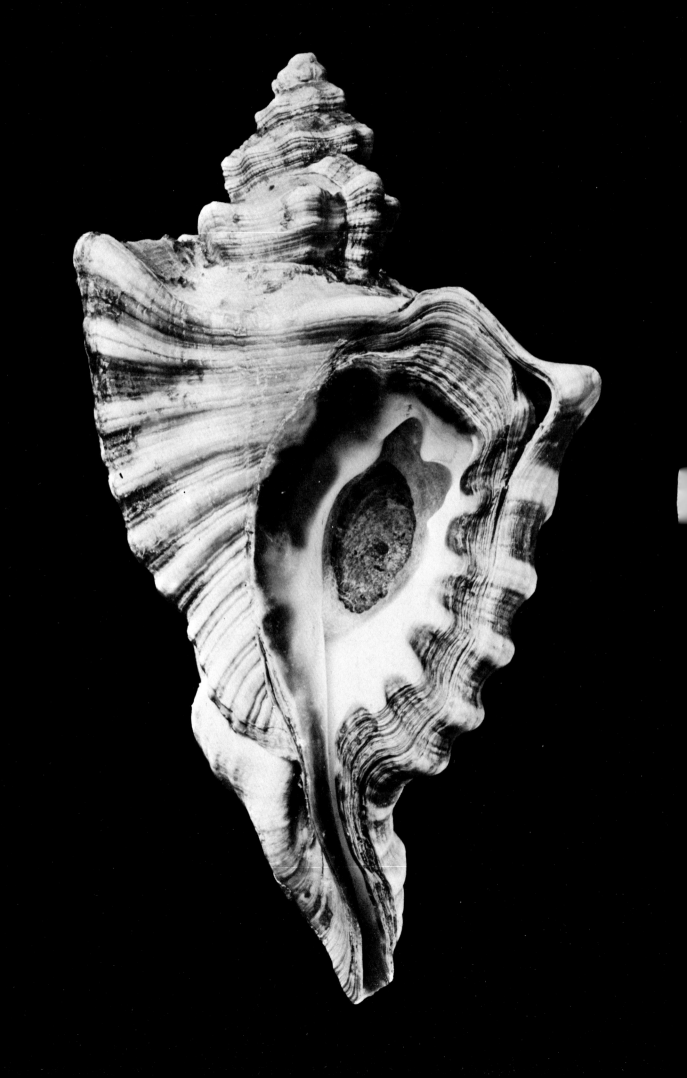

Rare Shells

We collect natural or artificial objects for many different reasons. Usually we like them or we believe we can profit from them commercially; sometimes both of these reasons are apparent to us. In most spheres of collecting we are drawn irresistibly towards the beautiful and the rare, and shell collectors have always been interested in specimens which are striking and difficult to obtain. Many species are rare in the sense that only one or two examples of each are known, but most of these are small and uninteresting to look at: each expedition which dredges material from the floors of the world's oceans brings to light numerous such shells. Collectors are interested in shells which are attractive as well as scarce; they want the exquisite cowries, cones, volutes, mitres, strombs, harps and other colourful and shapely species from the warm waters of tropical regions.

It is difficult to say when the 'rarity cult' began; one should perhaps exclude from the reckoning those shells which were treasured for reasons other than rarity and beauty. Palaeolithic tribes living in Central France travelled many miles to acquire seashells at the coast, but these were for personal adornment. A shell was likely to be picked up and kept if the finder knew that it could be perforated and subsequently strung onto a cord with other shells, teeth and bones to form a necklace. The Panther Cowries (*Cypraea pantherina*) found in Saxon graves in England, France and elsewhere in Europe were probably looked upon as fertility symbols, their natural beauty and their undoubted rarity at that time being factors of secondary importance. The Indian Chank (*Turbinella pyrum*) has been coveted for thousands of years—the exceedingly scarce reversed specimens particularly so—by Hindus, for whom these shells have a religious significance. But there is little or no interest in them as rare shells, and no-one has any regard for them as beautiful objects because they are anything but beautiful. Possibly the Greeks appreciated shells for what they were rather than for what they were supposed to signify. Certainly the Romans did. Excavations at Pompei, which was smothered by debris from the eruption of Vesuvius in 79 A.D., revealed a small collection of shells among which were cowries (*Cypraea pantherina, C. erosa*), a cone (*Conus textile*) and a pearl oyster (*Pinctada margaritifera*), shells which are certainly attractive. Bearing in mind the extent of western man's knowledge of the earth in the first century A.D., such shells from what was then considered the edge of the civilized world would have been uncommon and desirable objects in the estimation of their fortunate owner.

It is not until the late seventeenth century that we have a reference to a particular species being treasured solely for its rarity and beauty. The Precious Wentletrap (*Epitonium scalare*) was first brought to Europe from the East Indies in Dutch trading vessels and immediately it became a great

Collectors have always appreciated the graceful lines of the Precious Wentletrap (**Epitonium scalare**).

Previous pages **Cymatium ranzanii** *(left), a large gastropod from the eastern Indian Ocean, was almost unobtainable until recently. The Glassy Nautilus (**Carinaria cristata**) was once considered extremely valuable but is now of little interest to collectors. Despite its common name it is unrelated to the Paper Nautilus or to the Pearly Nautilus.* **Conus stupella** *is a recently discovered cone shell from Japanese waters.*

favourite with collectors. Large, perfect specimens were (and still are) in great demand and only the very rich could afford them. It is often stated that an estate was once given for a Precious Wentletrap in the seventeenth century, but this is highly improbable. In about 1750, however, Maria Theresa's husband gave 4,000 guilders for one (equivalent to several hundred pounds sterling). Some time during the nineteenth century rice-paste imitations are said to have been made by the

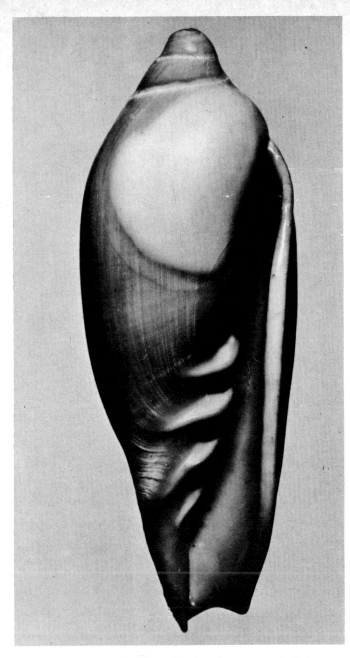

Afrivoluta pringlei, *the world's largest margin shell, from deep water off the Natal coast of South Africa*

were also in demand. A few of those species which were first acquired by Dutch collectors are still known by only a handful of specimens each. Most outstanding of these is the Great Spotted Cowry (*Cypraea guttata*) which has become easier to obtain only in recent years. From 1791, when it was described for the first time, until 1963 about 16 specimens were known to be in collections. Even today only affluent collectors can afford to buy specimens of this lovely shell.

The Glassy Nautilus (*Carinaria cristata*) was first made known from specimens collected around Amboina, at one time an important trading post in the former Dutch East Indies. Its popular name is based on a misconception. The extremely thin, fragile shell has a slight resemblance to that of the Paper Nautilus (*Argonauta argo*) but there the resemblance ends. It belongs to a totally unrelated mollusc which is several times too big for it. The creature floats about in the upper levels of the warmer seas, the shell being situated underneath. It was long considered to be the rarest of all shells and was very expensive until it began to go out of fashion in the early nineteenth century. Unlike the other shells mentioned in this chapter it is now considered unworthy of a place in the collector's cabinet.

What the Dutch did to reveal the conchological riches of the East Indies British navigators and their crews did for the Pacific. The voyages of Captain Cook and his colleagues encompassed several island groups never before explored by Europeans, and the many natural objects they acquired eventually became the prize possessions of collectors in Britain and elsewhere in Europe. It was from one of these voyages that the first specimens of the Golden Cowry (*Cypraea aurantium*) were made known. From the late eighteenth century until now no other shell has been so admired and coveted by collectors. The earlier specimens often had a small hole on one side and these still turn up in curio shops and at auctions. Such perforated specimens were once worn as ornaments in the hair, around the neck, or attached to the garments of high-ranking persons: most of them are said to have originated in the Fiji islands. Sometimes supernatural powers were attributed to them, and they were treasured as fetishes until well into the twentieth century. At no time has the Golden Cowry been out of favour, and it is now more popular than ever before. It is the undisputed showpiece of the cowries.

The Sun Shell (*Astraea heliotropium*), a striking shell from New Zealand, was brought to Europe at the same time as the Golden Cowry. For a time it was as popular, particularly when polished. Almost any of the more attractive shells from New Zealand and Australia were once considered rarities simply because they were unknown in Europe before the late eighteenth century.

Up to the end of the Napoleonic era relatively

Chinese for sale to those unable to buy (or unable to distinguish) the genuine shells. Such fakes are known, but it is unlikely that they were made in large numbers: the selling price could hardly have been sufficient to compensate for the labour and skill which must have gone into their manufacture. The Precious Wentletrap is no longer rare but it is still a favourite collectors' item and can be expensive to buy.

The Dutch were keen collectors of shells and other natural objects from the seventeenth century onwards and most of the early rarities were brought into Europe by them. From the East Indies came a number of species which were then considered desirable cabinet specimens. Indeed some of them are still costly and difficult to obtain. Cone shells were especially favoured, and cowries

few shells could be considered noteworthy for their rarity and beauty. Subsequently, with increasing knowledge of distant parts of the world, many striking novelties came to light. Rare volutes, cones and cowries—ever the collectors' favourites—came into circulation and ended up in the cabinets of amateurs who either did not know or did not care to record the locality of origin of their specimens. Consequently the provenance of many rarities remained unknown, often for very long periods. A few are almost impossible to obtain even now. Several volutes—*Festilyria festiva*, *Lyria lyraeformis* and *Aulica luteostoma*, for example—are among the most remarkable of the shells prized in the early nineteenth century. Many cones first publicized then are still scarce: *Conus cervus* and *C. crocatus* are, if anything, more difficult to find now than they were 150 years ago. The Prince Cowry (*Cypraea valentia*), the White-

Left   A large specimen of the Glory-of-India Cone **(Conus milneedwardsi)** *which was found in a fish basket at Tombean Bay, Mauritius, in the 1930's*

*Below   **Conus cervus**, a large cone shell from the Pacific. All the known specimens were collected before 1900.*

Opposite   Rumpf's Slit Shell **(Entemnotrochus rumphii)**

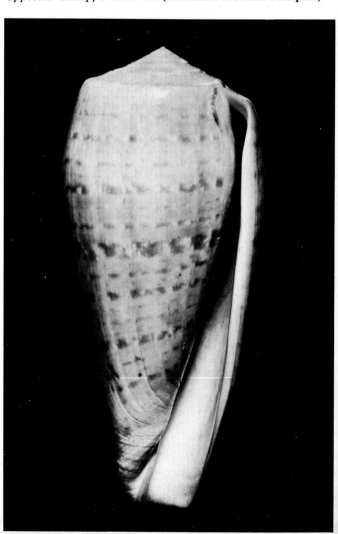

toothed Cowry (*Cypraea leucodon*) and the Surinam Cowry (*Cypraea surinamensis*) are outstanding rare cowries, the first two being among the most desirable of all seashells today. The beautiful Violet Spider Conch (*Lambis violacea*) has only just begun to come on the market in any quantity although it was known to science nearly two centuries ago.

The Glory-of-the-sea Cone (*Conus gloriamaris*) has always been much sought after from the time it first appeared in a European collection in the middle of the eighteenth century until the present day. It is not clear why it should have caught the popular imagination at all. It is attractive, but not exceptionally so: there are several closely similar cone shells and many more attractive ones which

receive only passing attention from collectors. Why it was given such a resounding name is not known, but doubtless this has contributed to its popularity.

Among the earliest-known specimens was one acquired by the fourth Earl of Tankerville at the London sale of the Duke of Calonne's collection in 1801. A large specimen in fine condition it was purchased on that occasion for 30 pounds. In 1825, when the earl's collection was due to be sold, a catalogue was drawn up, known as the *Tankerville Catalogue,* in which this shell was beautifully illustrated in colour. From then on, it seems, the Glory-of-the-sea was known to every shell collector

Above   Beyrich's Slit Shell (**Mikadotrochus beyrichi**), *a rare gastropod from Japanese waters*

Opposite   A fine specimen of the legendary Glory-of-the-Sea Cone (**Conus gloriamaris**)

and all aspired to own it. Most of those desiring to own one had no opportunity to see more than a coloured engraving and so their imagination filled in the details of its probable appearance.

In 1837 Hugh Cuming found two living specimens under a stone while collecting on a reef in the Philippines. As these were the first to be found

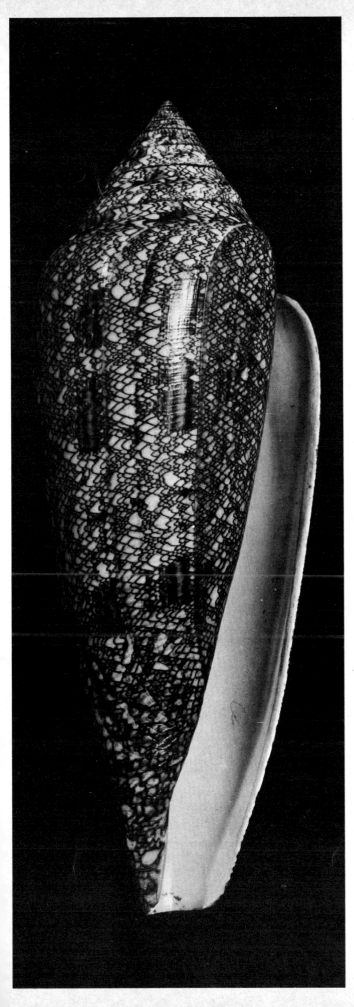

by a knowledgeable collector it is not surprising that he is said to have nearly fainted with delight. He nevertheless held the opinion that many of the shells he had collected in the Philippines were more valuable. It was subsequently reported that the reef on which he had found his specimens had been destroyed and that the Glory-of-the-sea had become 'as extinct as the Great Auk or Dodo'. It was many years before collectors were reassured that the world's most desirable shell was not extinct, for although one or two other examples were collected during the late nineteenth century it was not until 1957 that most collectors believed there was even a remote chance of acquiring one. In that year a Glory-of-the-sea was found in the Philippines and the discovery was widely reported in the popular press. Several others were found during the following decade and it became obvious that the species had a wide distribution in the Pacific. Very recently there was a trustworthy report of a haul of about 70 specimens having been found by a team of divers. This, perhaps, should have reduced the shell's appeal: it did nothing of the sort. Now that there is a real chance of obtaining a specimen collectors are just as eager, if not more so, to obtain one even though the price may still be relatively high. It may be a long time before this legendary shell ceases to fascinate collectors. Eventually it may come to hold a place in the affections of the collector similar to that now held by the Golden Cowry.

Unusual shells could sometimes turn up in the most unexpected situations. Perhaps the most unlikely place to find a large, beautiful and previously unknown shell is in a hotel bedroom, but that is where someone found the first specimen of Roadnight's Volute (*Pterospira roadnightae*). Baron von Müller, an eminent botanist, was staying at a hotel in Victoria, Australia, where he could not help noticing a specimen of this large, heavy volute propping open the window of his bedroom. He recognized it as being of potential scientific interest and eventually it came into the hands of Sir Frederick McCoy who, in 1881, described it as a new species totally distinct from all other molluscs. Apparently the landlord's mother, a Mrs. Roadnight, had found the shell on Ninety Mile Beach, Victoria. Mrs. Roadnight's discovery was all the more remarkable because the species is an inhabitant of fairly deep water.

Another striking shell was originally found in a place far removed from its deep-water habitat. Rumph's Slit Shell (*Entemnotrochus rumphii*) is now known to occur in deep water in the China Sea and neighbouring waters. Only in the past two or three years have specimens come onto the market and some of these are so big that they are impossible to overlook or to mistake for anything else. But the first one—still among the largest on record—to be noticed by a scientist was found by M. M. Schepman in a basket of miscellaneous

shells in Rotterdam. How this giant among shells was overlooked until the 1870's is a mystery. It is not so surprising that the first specimen of the less conspicuous Beyrich's Slit Shell (*Mikadotrochus beyrichi*) should have been discovered in a shell-work shop at Enoshima, Japan, in 1875.

At about this time a conchologist on holiday from England visited Barbados in the Lesser Antilles. One day he was looking in the window of a curio shop there and saw a large slit shell on a shelf. This turned out to be a fine specimen of Adanson's Slit Shell (*Entemnotrochus adansoniana*), then known by only one or two poorly preserved specimens. He went in and bought it, aware that this was the sort of thing that seldom

happens even once in a lifetime. The find was remarkable because this is a deep-water species which is never washed up on a beach. Several years later he went back to the same shop: there stood another, as large and as perfect as the first! Just how lucky Samuel Archer was is more readily appreciated when one learns that numerous well-equipped vessels have dredged extensively in that part of the world and only one or two specimens have been found by them.

Another source for rare shells is the underwater telegraph cable. Occasionally such cables have to be cleaned and it is surprising how much plant and animal life can be attached to them after a few years on the sea floor. In the later nineteenth and

Opposite   The Sun Shell **(Astraea heliotropium)** *from New Zealand was formerly a prized shell.*

Below   Roadnight's Volute **(Pterospira roadnightae),** *a large, rare volute from Australian waters*

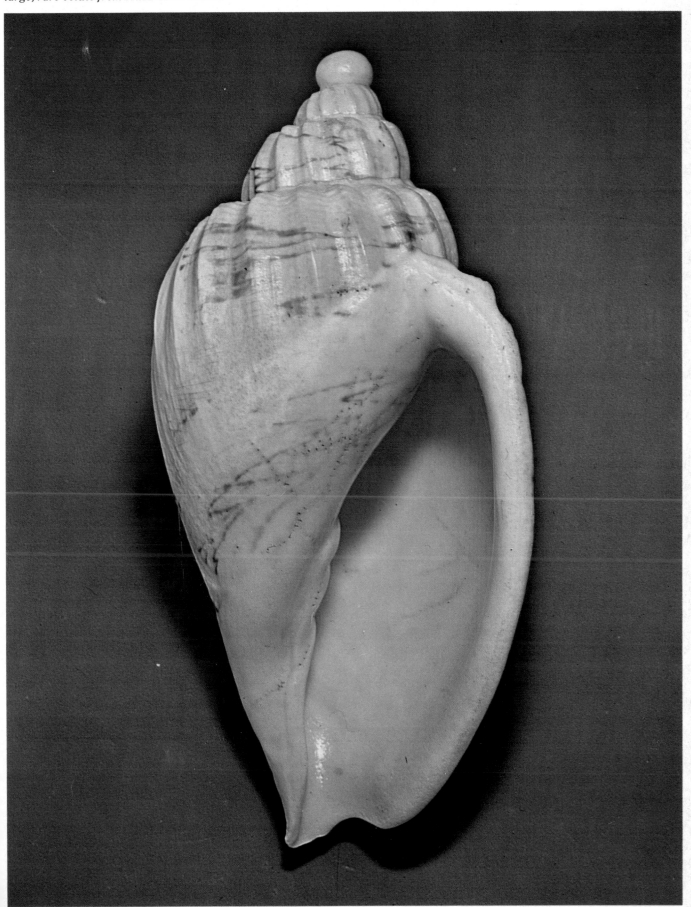

early twentieth centuries F. W. Townsend devoted much time to collecting material from encrusted cables and many valuable shells were retrieved by him. Most valuable by far were a few specimens of a cone which immediately became one of the most desirable of all shells. That shell is now known as the Glory-of-India Cone (*Conus milneedwardsi*). On one occasion in the 1890's Townsend safely netted two specimens and watched a third, much larger, fall back into the sea. Undoubtedly his regret at losing the third was only partially mitigated by his delight at securing the other two.

If Townsend was upset at losing such a fine shell how much greater must Samuel Stutchbury's disappointment have been earlier in the century. He was in a small boat dredging for shells in Sydney Harbour when an unusual bivalve shell attracted his attention. Placing it on the thwart of the boat he remarked to a companion that it must be a *Trigonia*. His companion laughingly reminded him that all the known species of *Trigonia* were fossils. Stutchbury, convinced that he had something of unusual interest, was about to inspect the shell when, as is the way of some bivalves, it leapt back into the water. He had indeed found a living fossil, now known as *Neotrigonia margaritacea*, and it was three months before he was able to find another specimen.

It must not be thought that all desirable and rare shells come from the sea. During the nineteenth century land and freshwater shells were considered very welcome additions to the collectors' cabinet. This is difficult to understand now, for only one non-marine shell—*Papustyla pulcherrima*,

Opposite One of the rarest marine bivalves, **Pholadomya candida**, *is known from a few specimens collected many years ago.*

Above The Glory-of-India Cone **(Conus milneedwardsi)**, *one of the most desirable shells. This specimen was collected off the Bombay coast in 1903 and is now in the National Museum of Wales.*

known as the Green Tree Snail because of its remarkable pea-green coloration—appeals to most collectors today. It was discovered in about 1930 on Manus Island north of New Guinea, where it lives in the foliage of trees. After the Second World War specimens became available in limited numbers and soon collectors were eager to have one or two to place alongside their seashells. Lately it has been gathered in such large numbers that import restrictions are now being imposed in some countries to prevent its extermination (although so far nothing has been done to stop anyone exporting it).

When exotic land and freshwater shells were in fashion with collectors one or two species were considered especially rare and brought high prices at auction. From Madagascar came a few specimens of a beautiful land shell, *Tropidophora deburghiae*. With the widespread destruction of the forests of Madagascar it is probable that it has been killed off along with many other remarkable shells for which that island was once famous. Most of the other land shells which used to be looked upon as outstanding rarities came from South America. *Newboldius crichtoni*, a shell of rather unprepossessing appearance, was known from only a single specimen for many years after it was originally described by a scientist early in the nineteenth century. It is still known from only a few specimens.

The most celebrated land shell rarity of all is *Sultana labeo*, known as the Blubber-lip Bulimus because of the singular appearance of its thick, apertural lip. This was first discovered on Christmas Day, 1827, in a farm house at about 8,000 feet, near Chachapoyas, Peru. The finder, Lieutenant Maw, saw other specimens in the vicinity, two of which were taken alive and given to a muleteer for safe keeping. The muleteer, mistaking them for articles of food, roasted them, ate the animals and, of course, destroyed the shells. Maw returned to England with a single shell and this was deposited in the museum of the Zoological Society in London. Soon afterwards this unique specimen was stolen and was never recovered. Many years later one or two other specimens turned up, but it was not until 1947 that someone revisited the original area and procured several good examples which he brought back to England. The discoverer found that the local inhabitants were accustomed to eating the animals after roasting them in their shells over an open fire. This little story helps to explain why a number of rare shells stay rare.

At the present time collectors, with one or two notable exceptions, are interested only in marine shells and there is constant competition between them to secure the rarer ones. With divers and fishermen on the look out for such shells all over the world it is not surprising that exquisite shells, some of them of extremely rare species, are being constantly brought into circulation.

Above **Tropidophora deburghiae** *(left) with* **Newboldius crichtoni** *(right)*

Opposite above The Green Tree Snail **(Papustyla pulcherrima)** *from Manus Island north of New Guinea*

Right **Neotrigonia margaritacea** *is a living species comparable to the fossil* **Trigonia** *shells.*

Shells and Man

Man's association with shells reaches back into prehistory. This is easy to understand when one considers that molluscs have always been a useful, and sometimes a vital, source of food. Enormous quantities are consumed annually even today, and not only by primitive peoples; oysters sustain the poor in some places but can be afforded only by the rich in others. It can hardly be doubted that initially man's appreciation of a shell was proportional to the size and flavour of the shell's occupant. As most molluscs are edible it follows that many different species were eaten. Primitive men and women would naturally have become fascinated by some of the shells they discarded, and eventually they would have realized their potential value as tools and, secondarily, as ornaments. It was to be a long time before anyone would want to collect them for the sheer pleasure they might give as non-utilitarian, non-decorative objects.

Undoubtedly mollusc eating was more popular in those far-off days than it is now. There is ample evidence to show that Neanderthal man habitually ate molluscs and sometimes cooked them. During Palaeolithic and Neolithic times their consumption by humans continued even though other food sources had become available. After the last of the Ice Ages there was a great increase in mollusc eating as is attested by the presence of large mounds of shells in many countries. In Japan, Denmark and California, mounds have been recorded which measure up to a mile or more in length, a half-mile or more in width, and 25 feet in depth! Few species are found in them, and some mounds contain only one. The species most often consumed vary from region to region: in the British Isles winkles were favoured, in Portugal otter shells, and in North America quahogs, oysters, mussels and various whelks. Not only marine molluscs were utilized. In Illinois, Missouri, Indiana and elsewhere in the United States large mounds of the shells of freshwater mussels and snails have been found; similar mounds have been found in Cambodia. Most of them were formed in prehistoric times but some are known to be of much more recent date.

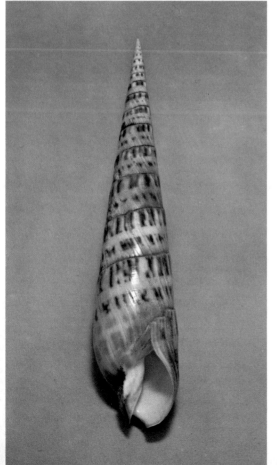

Opposite   Wayside stall in the Caribbean

Above   The Money Cowry (**Cypraea moneta**) *has been used as a currency in different parts of the world.*

Left   The Marlinspike (**Terebra maculata**), *a common Indo-Pacific shell, is sometimes used as a boring tool.*

Archaeological investigations in South-west France and elsewhere show clearly that shells came to be appreciated as objects of personal decoration during the Aurignacian period about 35,000 years ago. From this time onwards stone-age man decorated himself with shells which had been collected for that purpose. He polished them and pierced them so that they could be strung into necklaces and bracelets, together with seeds and animals' teeth and bones. The shells were the most important feature of these items: they may be considered the forerunners of the precious stones which replaced them many thousands of years later.

Most of the shells treated in this way were of edible molluscs, but some were not. Some pierced shells found in European caves and rock shelters were fossils which could only have been used for ornamental purposes. At European sites the two common winkles (*Littorina littoralis* and *Littorina littorea*) occur most frequently, many of them being pierced. Sometimes Mediterranean species are found and these may include a few fairly large shells. The presence of cowries and other comparatively scarce species at sites in Central France shows that primitive tribes wandered far in search of ornamental shells. The wearing of shell ornaments, even at this early date, was of wide occurrence and was as common in China as in France. It is surely remarkable that, in an age of space travel, many human beings still decorate themselves with shells in much the same way, and for nearly the same reasons, as their stone-age forbears did.

In tropical countries, where shells are much more numerous in number and kind, many intricate and sometimes beautiful articles have been produced. Cowries have been used by humans for many different things: head-dresses, bangles, belts, skirts, necklaces, octopus lures, bread-fruit scrapers, etc. In the Central Pacific, until recent times, the Golden Cowry was highly esteemed as an article of personal decoration by the natives and only persons of exalted rank were supposed to own them. Large quantities of margin shells (*Marginella*), which are particularly abundant off the coast of West Africa, were once used by tribesmen in the vicinity of Timbuktu, many miles from the sea.

The larger shells have occasionally been cut up into smaller pieces and used decoratively—cone shells are sometimes cut into rings which are strung together like beads or, if large enough, worn as amulets—but they usually serve more down-to-earth purposes. Large and voluminous shells have been used both to carry water and to get rid of it. The False Trumpet (*Syrinx aruana*) has been employed as a water carrier by natives of North Australia and New Guinea. A full-grown specimen weighing $4\frac{3}{4}$ pounds held $\frac{3}{4}$ gallon of water. A hole knocked in the body whorl, into which the thumb is inserted, is a necessary embellishment to facilitate carriage. Baler shells (*Melo*) have been used, as their name implies, to bale out water from canoes, though they have been put to many other uses too. Ladles and spoons have been fashioned out of small pieces of these shells; the thickened, and therefore stronger, parts of large shells have proved very useful where a particularly tough implement is required. Large auger shells (*Terebra*) are strong enough to be used in the natural state, and the Marlinspike (*Terebra maculata*) has often been used to penetrate substances softer than itself.

Bivalve shells have been employed in many different ways and those which are liberally lined with mother-of-pearl have always been preferred. Breastplates and smaller decorative items have been made from the large pearl oysters (*Pinctada*) of the Pacific and today designs are cut into the backs of these shells for sale to tourists. The Freshwater Pearl-mussel (*Margaritifera margaritifera*) was made into spectacle cases in Victorian times.

Wherever large gastropod shells occur, with the strange exception of Australia, men have found a use for them as trumpets. Certain shells, when perforated at or near the apex (occasionally in the body whorl near the aperture), are capable of producing a loud, booming noise when an expert blows into the hole. The resulting sound varies according to the type of shell, its size, and the expertise of the performer; it is sometimes as loud and as sonorous as a fog horn and may be heard several miles away. For this and other reasons shell trumpets have played an important part in man's affairs throughout the world.

In Polynesia it was customary to decorate large shell trumpets with human hair and human bones. Often a particular shell trumpet, such as the one owned by the famous King Kamehameha of Hawaii in the time of Captain Cook, was legendary and played a significant part in battles.

The Indian Chank (*Turbinella pyrum*) is a shell with a very special meaning in India. Its transformation into a shell trumpet is accomplished by simply knocking off its apex. But that is only a small part of the chank story, for here is a shell which has influenced the lives of millions of Hindus for many centuries. It is found only in the Indian Ocean and is especially common around the southern coast of India and around the Andaman Islands. For over two thousand years chanks have been collected in great quantities and used in various ways. Large numbers are still fished but the trade in chanks used to be very much greater; as many as four or five million were once shipped annually from the Gulf of Mannar between India and Ceylon.

Melo amphora, *a large baler shell. The coin beside the shell is a little over an inch across.*

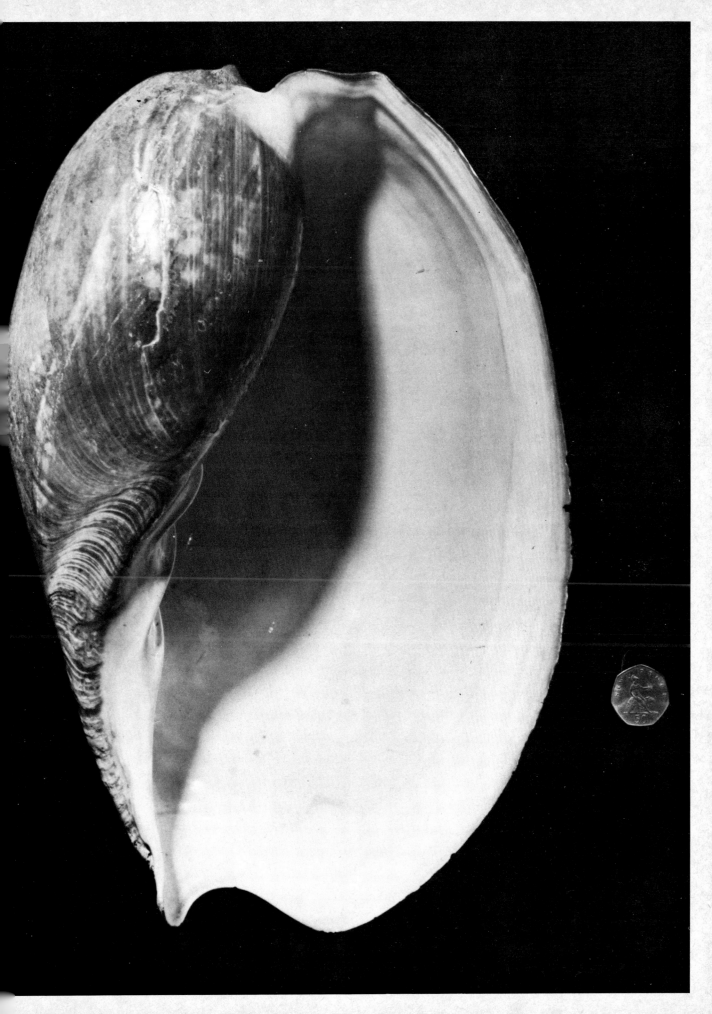

Above   A shell flower piece

Opposite above   A tun shell mounted on a gold stand

Right   Snuff box made from a cone shell mounted in silver

It is impossible to over-estimate the importance of the role played by the chank in a Hindu's life. In one form or another the shell crops up at every stage from birth, when he may be fed through a feeding spout made from one, to death, when he may go to his final resting place accompanied by loud blasts on a chank trumpet. Chank bangles are worn by brides instead of metal rings; beautifully lacquered and bejewelled bangles may be worn for personal adornment; a new home may have a complete shell buried in the foundations; and chank-bead necklaces and amulets may be worn as a protection against the evil eye and sickness. The number and variety of uses is limitless but it seems that the chank's original attraction was as a trumpet. In the early Indian epics, the Ramayana and Mahabharata, we find heroes encouraging their forces in battle with loud blasts on their trumpets each of which was fashioned from a chank. Every hero had his famous chank to which some high-sounding name was given: Eternal Victory, Sweet Voice, Lion's Roar and Jewel-blossom, to mention a few. King Arthur's sword, Excalibur, is the legendary equivalent of Panchajanya, the chank carried by Krishna. It is partly because Krishna, an incarnation of the god Vishnu, was closely associated with this shell that it came to have a religious significance.

A reversed chank is a prize indeed. Because it is extremely rare it is considered to be of special religious significance to a Hindu, so much so that specimens of the normally left-handed Lightning Whelk (*Busycon contrarium*) of Florida are currently being sold in India as cheap substitutes. Left-handed chanks encased in precious metal and set with precious stones are treasured relics in several Hindu temples.

Although it has played such an important part in the daily lives of many Indians for so long the chank has been used as a form of currency only by the Nagas of Assam (up to a century ago). Some other kinds of shell, however, have been used extensively in India and elsewhere for this purpose. Of these the Money Cowry is pre-eminent. This is not so surprising when one considers its conveniently small size, durability, wide distribution and abundance. Most of the other forms of shell money have been made, often very laboriously, from portions of shells of larger species. The principal source of these cowries used to be the Maldive and Laccadive Islands in the Indian Ocean where they still occur in untold millions. With them it was possible to buy a slave or to build a house; sometimes several millions were required to complete a transaction. In the early nineteenth century a European living at Cuttack on the north-east coast of India paid for the erection of his bungalow with shells, the price being 16 million cowries. It is also said that a church built in India, costing £4,000 sterling, was paid for in cowries: that would have been the equivalent of about 160 million cowries! In 1849 nearly 300 tons of them were brought to the English port of Liverpool. Ships carrying such cargoes have been wrecked in places far distant from the original habitats of these shells, and this accounts for the occasional discovery of tropical cowries on beaches far outside the tropics. In the year 1873, for instance, a ship bound for Liverpool from Manila was wrecked off the Cumberland coast of England. On board were 600 bags of cowries. For many years afterwards cowries were being picked up on the nearby shores and gave some of the finders the idea that the species was native to Britain.

There were numerous other kinds of shell currency. That of the Indians living along the Atlantic coast of North America was derived from a heavy bivalve variously called the Hard-shell Clam, the Round Clam, or the Quahog (*Mercenaria mercenaria*). The inside of each valve is stained purple around the margin. It was the stained part which the Indians valued most; this part was broken off and converted into beads which were then strung together. The white portion of the shell (and of other whitish shells) served as currency of lesser value, known as 'wampum'. Very different shells were employed by Indians of the west coast of North America. Tusk-shell money was in common use from Alaska to California. The shells were made up into elaborate strings, the length of which determined the value. Abalone money, made from one of several species (*Haliotis rufescens, H. splendens*, or *H. cracherodei*), was elegant by comparison, the shells of these species being susceptible to polishing. Many worked fragments of these shells have been found in old Indian burial mounds. Mention should also be made here of the use of large land shells as forms of currency, particularly in Africa. The shells of the Giant African Snail (*Achatina fulica*) and its allies are worked up into small discs and strung on long lengths of string. Obviously such shells were more easily obtained by tribes living far in the interior for whom seashells were rare luxuries.

It may seem unlikely that there should be a connection between molluscs and the beautiful purple-coloured robes worn since time immemorial by kings, queens and other persons of high rank; but the connection is close. Some molluscs produce a fluid resembling thick cream in colour and consistency which, on exposure to light, undergoes a progressive colour change from white, through yellow, green, blue and red, to purple (it may adopt many other shades of colour within that range). A long time ago (4,000 years would be a conservative estimate) it was discovered that cloth impregnated with this substance retained its colour almost indefinitely and could resist repeated washings and exposure. As purple dye from this source is not only permanent but beautiful also, it is small wonder that human beings came to regard it highly and eventually reserved its use

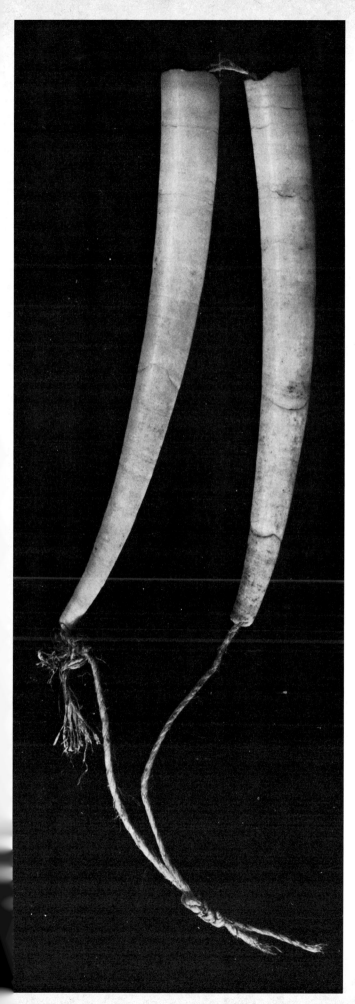

for the very wealthy or for those of high rank.

Many marine gastropods can produce a dye which will stain cloth permanently but only a few species are large enough and abundant enough to have been worth founding an industry upon. In the Mediterranean, the region where the use of 'royal purple' was exploited most energetically, two species were used almost exclusively: the Straight-spined Murex (*Bolinus brandaris*) and the Banded Murex (*Hexaplex trunculus*). There is plenty of evidence to show that these were the principal sources of royal purple. Mounds containing incalculable numbers of such shells have been found in many coastal districts of the Mediterranean, particularly around the eastern coast. Such mounds may still be seen by the old walls of Sidon, and there are many others along the Syrian coast. The economy of the Phoenicians seems to have been greatly dependent upon the production of purple-dyed cloth, and their well-known skill in navigating merchant craft anywhere from the Black Sea to southern Spain and Britain certainly helped to expand their monopoly of the trade in this highly desirable commodity.

There is a simple explanation for the astronomical number of shells contained in these mounds. Each snail produces such a tiny amount of the dye that it was necessary to process huge numbers of them to obtain sufficient to colour a small garment. A modern man's neck-tie would require the juices to be extracted from about 10,000 specimens of the Straight-spined Murex. It is said that Cleopatra's fleet sailed into action at Actium with all-purple sails. If the story is true an astronomical number of molluscs had to be sacrificed for what must indeed have been a most colourful enterprise. Processing the molluscs was a lengthy, dirty and smelly business. Smaller shells were crushed and the juice extracted. Larger shells were broken open individually in such a way that the gland containing the precious fluid was exposed and could be removed by hand. The smell of the freshly extracted juice is unpleasant being similar to a mixture of bromine gas and garlic. Consequently the vats in which the processing was carried out were usually situated down-wind from the town.

Outside of the Mediterranean region the use of purple dye extracted from molluscs has not been so important or so highly organized. In western Britain the Dog Whelk (*Nucella lapillus*) provided the early Britons with a similar, though less brilliant, dye with which they coloured their garments and occasionally themselves. On the west coast of Central America and the north-west coast of South America the Wide-mouthed Purpura

A pair of tusk shells strung together and used as native currency

H.matisse 53

(*Purpura patula pansa*) was used for dyeing cotton in prehistoric times. Even now the same species is used to dye cotton threads by the Tehuantepec Indians of Mexico. The value of the dyeing fluid to a mollusc is not well understood at the present time. Perhaps it has a defensive purpose because it is known to be distasteful to fish, and the egg capsules of the dye-producing molluscs, which have a high concentration of this substance, are not eaten by fish or other would-be predators.

Above **The Snail** *by Matisse*

Opposite   The graceful curves and spirals of a tun shell are revealed by this X-ray photograph.

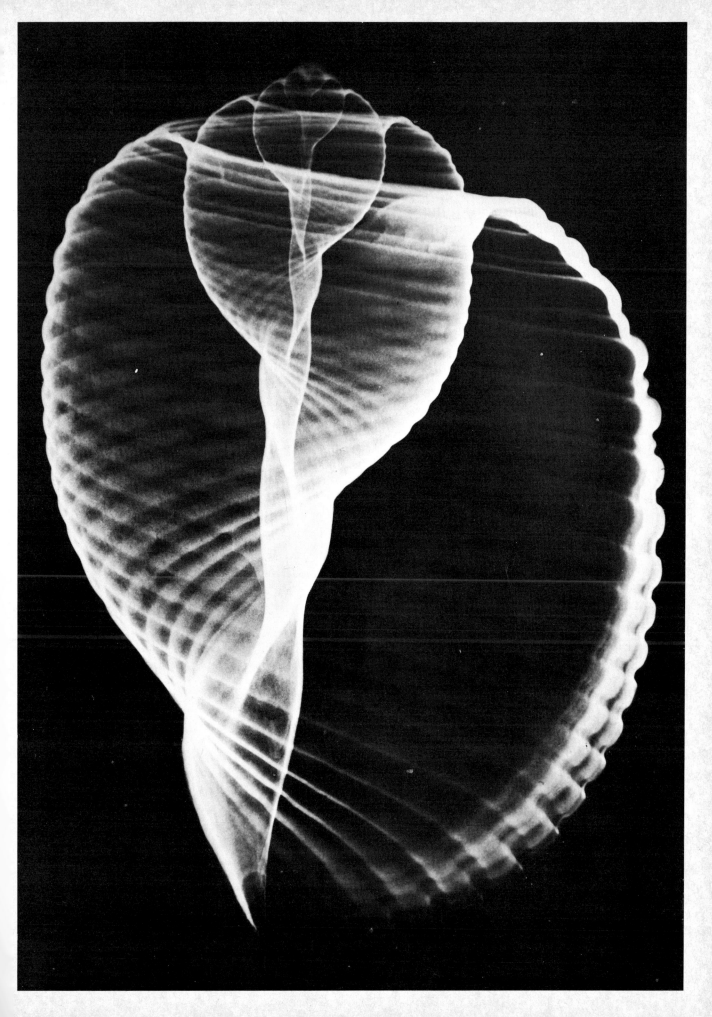

Shells and Art

Long before shells and their inmates became of scientific interest they were appreciated for their beauty. Their shapes, sculpture, colours and colour patterns compelled attention. Primitive men and women, who wore pierced shells, also discovered that they could alter the appearance of shells to suit their fancy. In its simplest form this could be achieved by making scratch marks on a shell's surface with a sharp instrument, or by decorating it with various stains. By filing, cutting and abrading the shell it was possible to alter its overall shape. We cannot tell at what point any of these activities can be said to have produced a work of art: that would be to define a work of art. Shell artifacts were produced for various purposes, mostly functional or decorative, but some can be regarded as the result of a primitive urge to create something aesthetically pleasing.

We marvel at the beautiful representations of animals painted on the walls of caves at Lascaux and Altamira. Those much smaller pictures, usually of animals or humans, scratched on stones, bones and shells, are equally examples of artistic expression. We must allow that, in the context of their time, the representation of a reindeer or a mammoth on a shell is a work of art, no matter how crude the execution of it. If we do not make this allowance then we should not accept as art those superb engravings on shells executed by European craftsmen many centuries later. The *Nautilus* shells, engraved by members of the Bellekin family in the sixteenth and seventeenth centuries, are exquisite examples of an art form which is peculiarly Dutch. They are also examples of an art form which is rooted in antiquity.

Crude scratches or delicate toolwork on shells produce skin-deep effects which differ widely in degree but not in kind. Different in degree also is the shell cameo, another art form which has come down to us from the distant past. Shell cameos are pictorial carvings in the outer layers of certain shells which may be left in their original place or removed, and mounted and worn as pendants, brooches or rings. It would, however, be more correct to describe them as small-sized sculptures executed in low relief on a substance precious for its beauty, its rarity or its hardness, and preferably all three. The purist would show little interest in a cameo which had not been cut upon a jewel or an onyx.

In the British Museum there is a cameo, cut in amethyst, showing a recumbent lion. It dates from about the sixth or seventh century B.C. and may be Mycenaean in origin. A simple cameo, cut in the shell of a large bivalve of the genus *Tridacna,* is also in the British Museum and is of comparable age to the other cameo. A shell cameo of such great antiquity is rare indeed. The widespread use of shells for cameo carving is of relatively recent origin, and the art of carving them reached its zenith in the nineteenth century.

When using a shell the craftsman's objective is to take advantage of its layered structure to produce a relief effect, the middle layer being of a different colour to those above and below. Cameo work flourished in Italy for many centuries and the best shell cameos (and many of the worst) are still being made there. Italian craftsmen came to England to work and one of the best, Ronca, became cameo-maker to Queen Victoria. Some of the most exquisite shell cameos ever made were Ronca's handiwork and are highly prized by their present owners.

The cameo was carved from a suitable part of the shell and, when finished, was cut out and mounted. Alternatively, the carving was left in its place on the shell. This was the usual practice with carvings executed on large shells or on shells with thin layers. The subject matter of the smaller cameos was usually a profile of a classical hero or heroine and special attention was given to the details of coiffure and drapery. Larger cameos had for their subjects classical scenes, mostly taken from Greek mythology.

Outside Europe shell cameos have usually taken cruder and simpler forms. Some are delightful but most of them are not intended to be anything more than knick-knacks for tourists. The Bull's-mouth

Below Cameo carved in the surface layers of a Tiger Cowry

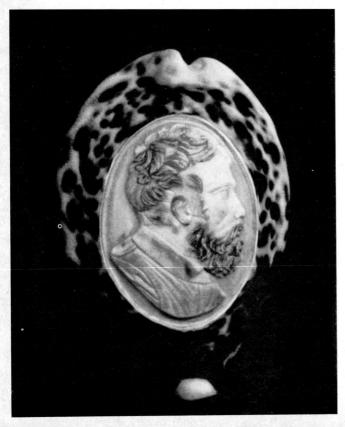

Previous pages Still-life with shells by Bosschaert

Opposite Italian renaissance wall pendant with shell motifs

Conch (*Cassis rufa*) from the West Indies is the cameo cutter's favourite material, and by far the greater number of existing shell cameos have been cut from it. Large cameos were usually carved on shells of the Emperor Helmet (*Cassis madagascariensis*), also a West Indian species. A humbler form of cameo carving was executed on shells of the Tiger Cowry (*Cypraea tigris*). In bric-a-brac stores it is still possible to pick these up embellished with the Lord's Prayer.

Shells can be used by themselves or in other ways in conjunction with other natural or artificial objects, to produce works of art. The nacreous inner lining of many shells has been put to a myriad uses by craftsmen. Objects made of, or incorporating 'mother-of-pearl' (a term descriptive of any piece of shell having a nacreous or pearly gleam) have delighted human beings, savage and civilized, for centuries. Among the countless uses of mother-of-pearl may be mentioned inlay work of all kinds, ranging from articles of furniture to snuff boxes, functional items such as buttons, combs and knife handles, and luxury items such as spectacle cases, scent bottles, playing-card cases

and fans. Sometimes it is necessary only to rub down the surface of a shell to reveal the mother-of-pearl gleam below, and such shells are often considered artistic objects in their own right. Some large shells, in particular turban shells (*Turbo*), were at one time encased in precious metal and mounted as ornamental drinking cups.

This is not the place to discuss the uses of pearls in art but, as they are familiar by-products of molluscs, they cannot be ignored altogether. The products of natural or artificially stimulated irritation between the mantle and inner shell of certain bivalves, pearls have been coveted by men and women since prehistoric times. The best pearls are found in the large Pacific Pearl Oyster (*Pinctada maxima*), although other marine bivalves may produce good ones. Even the Freshwater Pearl Mussel (*Margaritifera margaritifera*) of Europe and North America occasionally produces pearls of outstanding quality. Pearls obtained from the mussels of the River Conway in Wales were once so famous that they were said to be one of the reasons for Julius Caesar's invasion of Britain. A number of perfectly matched or graded

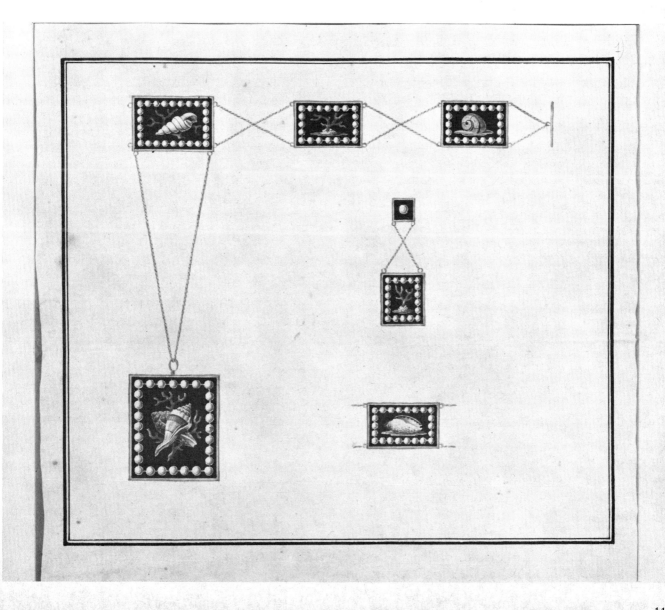

pearls may be used to make a beautiful necklace or collar, and it would be difficult not to consider these as works of art. Sometimes the craftsman took advantage of the contours of a deformed baroque pearl to create a brooch or pendant of unusual design and great beauty.

All those items of shell bric-a-brac which were made to grace so many homes in Victorian England and elsewhere are also worthy of note. Elaborate flower arrangements, composed principally of shells, were exhibited under glass domes close to similarly covered displays of humming birds and other exotic fancies. If they were not destined to be classified as great works of art it was not for want of trying. The better displays required many hours of patient and skilful preparation.

The shell grotto—product of an earlier age when every grand house in England had its grotto with its resident hermit—should also be mentioned. The grotto, or artificial cave, was made of rocks, crystals, moss, weeds, shrubs and exotic shells— the whole presenting a suitably romantic appearance. One of the most meticulously constructed grottoes was that built at Goodwood Park, Sussex, by the Duchess of Richmond and her two daughters. They had been at their self-appointed task for seven years when the decoration of the grotto was completed in 1746.

Three-dimensional art objects using naturalistic shell forms occur in many different contexts. In the world of ceramics few names are more celebrated than that of Bernard Palissy, the Huguenot potter, glass painter and naturalist. His ceramic ware was often ornamented with life-like copies of animals and plants, and shells provided him with ideas for some of his most attractive pieces. This is not surprising as he was a competent naturalist who lectured on shells and had a small collection of them.

Among the ceramic wares of later centuries may be mentioned those of certain factories in the British Isles, such as those at Derby, Worcester and Burslem. Less famous than these is the porcelain factory at Belleek in County Fermanagh, Ireland, which has been manufacturing fine-quality pieces finished with a remarkably lustrous glaze since the middle of the nineteenth century. Naturalistic shell designs occur on many Belleek items. The mounted Argonaut, or Paper Nautilus, was a favourite with these factories. Josiah Wedgwood's Etruria works at Burslem near Stoke-on-Trent concentrated on the production of high-quality wares which followed classical patterns. Among the simpler items he produced was an Argonaut-shaped wall bracket overlaid with purple. Belleek ware favours the use of a cockle-shell motif in the designs of cups, saucers, plates and other items, the details of the shells' sculpture being so faithfully reproduced that it is possible to

Above   Early nineteenth-century wall pocket made by Wedgewood in moonstone lustre

Opposite   Beleek sweetmeat dish manufactured in 1868

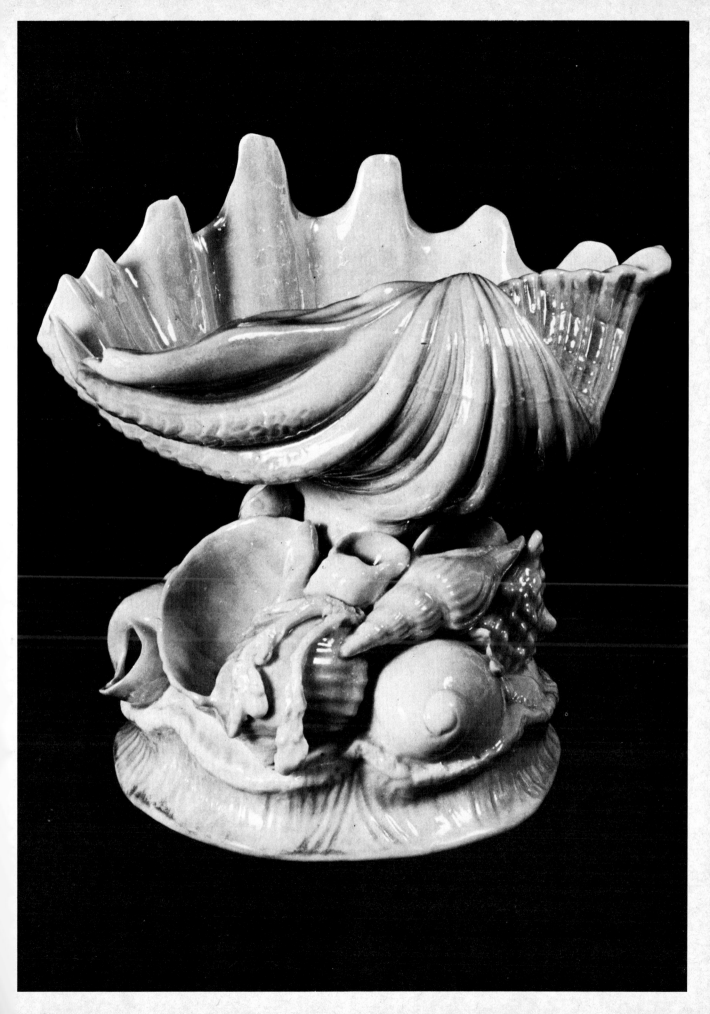

Botticelli's **Birth of Venus**

identify the species which served as artist's models.

Though his work is all two-dimensional, it is appropriate to mention here the art of the china painter, Thomas Baxter. In the early nineteenth century he worked at several factories and painted exquisite pictures of animals, feathers, plants and seashells as well as landscapes on plates, saucers, cups, etc. His shell paintings vary in quality, but at their best they are unsurpassed. A plate painted by him when he was working at the Swansea factory shows a number of shells then considered very rare. It is a very beautiful piece indeed and cannot be faulted artistically or scientifically. The shells were evidently drawn from life and must have been part of a fine collection. The owner of the Swansea factory at that time was Lewis Weston Dillwyn, who was a keen conchologist and author of a descriptive catalogue of shells. Perhaps he was instrumental in obtaining the shells for Baxter to paint.

One kind of shell, the scallop, occurs in so many different art forms that it could claim a chapter to itself. Because it was associated with Aphrodite, the Greek goddess of love, and Venus, her Roman equivalent, it has been widely adopted as a symbolic motif and has become enshrined (sometimes literally) in many architectural structures as well as in countless smaller and often portable items, such as statuettes, coins and brooches. In stylized form the scallop makes a very pleasing motif when executed in deep relief. The scalloped niches used in many buildings, altars and large tombs all stem directly from the Venus-rising-from-the-scallop tradition. The scallop motif has been used for centuries in the manufacture of domestic utensils, especially fruit dishes, trays and moulds. Scent bottles resembling scallops have also been dug up at Roman sites.

What was originally a symbol has become a convention which is still in daily use all over the world. This is understandable in aesthetic terms because the scallop lends itself to many imaginitive interpretations, whether in wood, stone, metal or paper. What was once a symbol of fruitfulness and emblematic of the sea is now more familiar as the trade mark of a large company which trades in oil. Such dissimilar people as Botticelli, Marcus Samuel and Sir Winston Churchill have something in common: the scallop. Botticelli's most famous painting shows Venus standing on one in mid-ocean. Samuel, a co-founder and the first chairman of the Shell Oil Company, originally traded in shells, hence the well-known trade mark. Winston Churchill joins their company on the strength of the scallops which grace his coat of arms.

Certain gastropod shells have been as fruitful a source of artistic inspiration as the scallop. One or two of the salient features of the gastropod shell, especially its spiral configuration, are echoed in some of our more celebrated buildings. Conchologists are often tempted to assume a connection between the architectural designs of some Japanese buildings and certain gastropod shells found commonly in Japanese waters. Since the Japanese have been interested in shells for centuries it is just possible that they drew inspiration from them when planning their pagodas and temples. The aptly-named Common Pagoda Shell (*Columbarium pagoda*) acquires its popular name from its resemblance to pagoda-like buildings, but it cannot be assumed that early Japanese architects used it as a model. It is also tempting to suggest that the Japanese Wonder Shell (*Thatcheria mirabilis*) inspired a Japanese architect long ago.

It is, perhaps, more excusable to suspect a real rather than an imagined connection between some gastropod shells and a few very old European buildings. Most striking is the similarity between some spiral staircases and the internal structure of several familiar gastropod shells. At Venice, in the Palazzo Contarini, there is a beautiful staircase known as the Scala del Bovolo. Even a person with no knowledge of shells cannot fail to see a remarkable similarity between it and a conical shell such as the Precious Wentletrap. The beauty of the handrail and the pillared arches is enhanced by their following the line of an ascending spiral. The successive tiers of the Leaning Tower of Pisa are uninteresting by comparison simply because they do not follow an ascending spiral.

At Fiesole, in the convent of San Domenico, there is a flight of eight steps leading down to the cloister which is so arranged that it is known as the 'Scala della Conchiglia' (the 'Staircase of the Shell'). The 'Escalier de la Reine Berthe' at Chartres, when viewed from the outside, is strongly reminiscent of the shell of a large mitre, such as the Papal Mitre (*Mitra papalis*). From one viewpoint the pointed roof simulates the apex of this shell, and the doorway resembles its shadowy aperture.

The internal folds or plaits which wind around the columella of volutes, mitres and many other gastropod shells are also matched by similar structures inside some of these old staircases. A staircase in the Old Wing of the Château of Blois has a central pillar which is encircled by a stone handrail. The resemblance to the single plait encircling the columella of certain shells is strikingly evident when the shells are sectioned.

Among modern examples of architecture in which an ascending spiral is cleverly employed is the Solomon R. Guggenheim Museum, New York, in which works of art are displayed. It was designed by the great American architect, Frank Lloyd Wright, who is known to have made a close

Jan Gossaert's **Neptune and Amphitrite**. *Neptune's shell may be* **Charonia lampas,** *a Mediterranean species. Amphitrite wears a scallop in her hair.*

study of shell structure. Despite the similarity of these architectural and conchological features the resemblances appear to be mostly fortuitous. The buildings and the shells are constructed according to designs which give strength and harmony to the whole. A minimum of material gives maximum support. For once man and nature appear to have found identical solutions to identical problems.

Shells have been an endless source of inspiration to painters although they are rarely introduced for other than pictorial effect. Botticelli's allegorical pictures are, of course, outstanding exceptions. We have already mentioned his picture of the birth of Venus, but he also painted an 'Allegory of the Shell', showing two men carrying a stylized Straight-spined Murex (*Bolinus brandaris*) from the aperture of which protrudes a man holding a snake.

Non-allegorical and non-symbolic pictures illustrating shells were painted in the Low Countries from the sixteenth to the eighteenth centuries. Still-lifes by Jan van Kessel, Balthasar van der Ast, Jean Baptiste Bosschaert and others include shells arranged decoratively as festoons, floral displays, and so on. Occasionally a shell would be incorporated into a picture where it played a minor role to fill up a vacant space. Rembrandt was content to reproduce a simple but eloquent etching of a Marbled Cone (*Conus marmoreus*),

now known as 'The Little Horn'. Since he forgot to reverse the spiral coiling of the shell on the metal plate, the etching shows a sinistral shell; but it scarcely matters.

Modern painters have taken more notice of shells as objects conveying hidden meanings. In his childhood James Ensor, the Belgian painter, was accustomed to see shells all around him because members of his family, who owned shops in Ostend, traded in them. Many of his pictures show shells of all shapes and sizes grouped with the skeletons, skulls and masks which he so loved to portray. Matisse's painting 'The Snail' is considered to be a major example of that artist's work and Joan Miró's 'Composition with Shell', in which prominence is given to a real scallop shell, is another notable modern painting. The significance of these paintings is not immediately clear, but perhaps Rembrandt said all that needed to be said in his etching and has left little for his successors to add except mystery.

Below   Rembrandt's etching of a Marble Cone. Because Rembrandt failed to engrave it as a mirror image the shell appears reversed.

Opposite   Statue of Hermes by Jacopo Sansovino in the Loggetta di San Marco, Venice

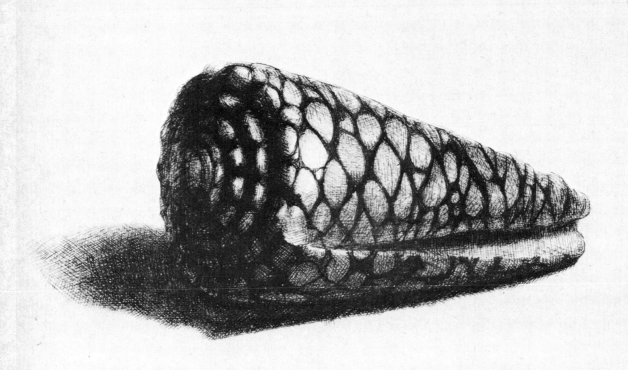

Index

Acknowledgements

Numbers in italic refer to colour plates. American Museum of Natural History, New York: 92 left; Heather Angel: 6–7, 9, 12, 16, *17 bottom*, 18, 19, *20 top*, 22–23, *32 top right*, 37 bottom; Ardea Photographics: 10 top, *20 bottom right*, 26 top & bottom, 27, 30, 33, 34 left, 36, 37 top, 41 top, 44 top & bottom, 45, 46 top left, 51, 55 left, *56 top*, 58 top, *66*, 85, 86, 96, *100*, 107, 111, 116, (P.J. Green); Author *28–29*, 35, *38–39*, *49 bottom*, 55 right, *61*, 62–63, 64, 68–69, *70*, 72–73, *75*, 77 bottom, 82–83, 88 left, 88–89, 90, (R. Winckworth Collection), 91, 92 right, 93, 94, 95; Alice Denison Barlow: End-papers, *25 left*, *32 bottom*, *56 bottom*, *78 top & bottom*, 79 top & bottom, 97, 101 top & bottom, 105 top & bottom; Barnaby's Picture Library, London: back jacket; The Belleek Pottery Ltd, Co. Fermanagh, Ireland: 119; B.P.C. Publishing Ltd: *108, 109 bottom left*, (Private Collection); J. Allan Cash, London: 104; Bruce Coleman Ltd: *17 top* (Allan Power), Title page, *25*, 31, (Jane Burton). 42 top, *49 top left*, *60 top*, (Rob Bock); Linnean Society, London: 68, 69, 71; Mansell Collection, London: 76; Museum d'Histoire Naturelle de la Ville de Geneve: 41 bottom, 113; The Natural History Photographic Agency: 42 right, 46–47. (A. Bannister), *21*, *24*, *57*, *67*. (J. M. Clayton), 8, 23 right, 34 right, 43, 48, *60 bottom right*. (L. Jackman), 10 bottom left, 11; National Museum of Wales: 14–15, 58 bottom, 89 right, 98, 99; Picturepoint Ltd, London: 102–103; Rijksmuseum, Amsterdam: 124; Dr. Norman Runham: 13; Scala, Florence: *109*, 114–115, 117, 120–121, *125*; State Museum, Berlin-Dahlem: 23; Syndication International, London: 74; Tony Taylor: *Front jacket*, *52–53*; Trustees of the British Museum (Natural History), 75 (Banks Collection), 77 top (Soane Collection); Trustees of the Tate Gallery, London: *112*; Josiah Wedgewood & Sons Ltd: 118; © S.P.A.D.E.M. Paris, 1972: *112*.